MW00426676

i

© 2018 BC Movie, LLC

SHAMANISM IN THE NEW MILLENNIUM

All rights reserved. No part of this publication may be reproduced, stored in a retrieval system or transmitted in any form or by any means, electronic, mechanical, photocopying, recording or other- wise without the prior permission of the publisher or in accordance with the provisions of the Copyright, Designs and Patents Act 1988 or under the terms of any license permitting limited copying issued by the Copyright Licensing Agency.

Published by: Rampant Feline Media/BC Movie, LLC

Cover Design by: Suzette Maffi

ISBN-13: 978-0-9998354-0-1
Distributed by: Ingram Spark

Table of Contents

SECTION III - Modern Applications

INTRODUCTION

Back in 2008 when I was first introduced to the powerful gift of plant medicine by Peruvian shaman Rossana Nascimento (whose chapter opens this book), I was deeply impacted—not just in terms of personal healing and insights, which were many, but also by the dedication and profound knowledge of the men and women guiding the ceremonies. As I penetrated more deeply into my own psyche and cellular matrix (and more deeply into the jungles of the Amazon), being a journalist, I couldn't help but be curious about shamanic training and the astoundingly rich heritage my guides were heir to, the benefits of which I was reaping.

Over the many weeks that we worked, traveled and lived together, a friendship with Rossa grew. I started asking questions about her training. And I was stunned by what I learned: How a young apprentice (and I mean young!) would be sent into the jungles to live alone for up to a month ingesting one plant, discovering from the plant itself what its qualities and potentials were when taken in the morning, the evening, during the waxing of the moon, the waning, at full and at full dark, raw, cooked, steamed, boiled, roots and leaves and stems. After a full month of this diet, they would stagger out of the jungle back to camp, weak and disoriented—but oh, so much wiser. A month of recovery, working ceremonies, learning the healing arts at the side of their teacher, then back out into the jungle they would go with yet another plant.

This kind of experiential training went on for *decades*.

At the same time as I was learning about the depth, dedication and unbelievable sacrifice involved in shamanic training in the Amazon, I was witness to an influx of students from the US and Europe—serious investigators of shamanic work also willing to dedicate decades to the craft—along with what I can only call "shaman wannabees" flooding into the Amazon and towns like Iquitos, seeking out shamans for training, staying for short periods of time then departing, thinking they had acquired wisdom. Equally unsettling was watching "spiritual teachers" arrive with their flocks of followers who had paid thousands of dollars or euros each for the privilege of working with a shaman who was often paid, at best, a couple hundred dollars per ceremony.

Saddened by the all-too-frequent exploitation of this extraordinary and rapidly disappearing resource, I determined to write a book about shamanism, exposing what it *really* takes to be able to hang out a shingle with the "S" word on it. And then life happened. I wrote several books (none on shamanism) and the years passed swiftly. Then, my friend, author and filmmaker Betsy Chasse, called me with the idea of publishing a compilation book on shamanism. Would I be the book's editor?

I leapt at the chance.

The result is not a definitive look at shamanic traditions from around the world. That would take a lifetime and require an encyclopedia. What it is, is an exploration of shamanism through the stories of sixteen individuals revealing how a person is called by Spirit (often reluctantly) to become a healer, what that journey looks like from multiple perspectives and traditions, what becoming a shaman/healer entails, and how that journey is transforming in the face of rapid cultural changes, loss of traditions, loss of ecosystems, and the loss of interest in "the old ways."

The book itself is organized in a directional flow, starting with the stories of women and men trained in ancient traditions, bridging into stories of transition where training and outlook blend old and new, finally arriving at the place where the "heartbeat"—the essence—of the shamanic healing art shines through intimate tales of healers who no longer even use the word "shaman" to describe themselves and what they do.

It has been an honor to be involved in this project, and I have been deeply moved by all of the stories in this book and what they reveal. I hope you will be as well.

Cate Montana
Editor

SECTION I
Traditional Voices

CHAPTER 1

Rossana Nascimento is an Amazonian Traditionalist Shaman who has spent more than 30 years researching the Ayahuasca CosmoVision and the interpretation of its deep hiden messages. An expert in Amazonian plant detoxification protocols and Ayahuasca therapy, she is a natural-born intuitive healer. Born into a traditional shamanic family in the Amazon regions of Peru, she began living the shaman's life in childhood. Today, her work as a shaman, spiritual healer and coach/trainer, workshop facilitator, and ceremonial leader, is based on the indigenous practices of her ancestors. She gives personalized assistance to individuals seeking deep transformation in their lives, helping many people to transform and asimilate changes in their lives in a highly positive way. She facilitates private sessions, lectures, classes, workshops, and spiritual rituals as well as national and international retreats and shamanic conferences. Rossa has been a featured speaker at major events, shamanic congresses, festivals and conferences worldwide.

For more information please go to www.rossana-nascimento.com or write her at rossananascimento@hotmail.com

Banned Magic and Mysterious Rituals in the Heart of the Amazon Jungle

An Ayahuasca CosmoVision is an open door to the Universal Cosmic World. It's the key that opens multidimensional doors, supplying the answer to all your spiritual questions, giving you a wisdom that goes into the deepest unknowns of this magic, mystic world.

The moment you get to understand that all of life—down to the smallest seed or grain of sand—is part of the order of the universe and that the universe is inside you, every picture or figure you see, every sensation you may feel suddenly has a message for you, a code that can be interpreted for you to be able to understand those messages and apply them to this world and your life.

Unfortunately, the vast majority of people in the modern-day world never have the chance to hold such a vision or embrace that kind of wisdom. They don't even think of the possibility. Then life puts them in front of the sudden possibility of death. They are tormented by a terminal disease, fearful of death. Or they despair of fear itself and weep over the vision of an empty life without any reason to live.

In moments like this, we fall into a state of deep depression. In times like these our innate survival instincts force us to look for a way out. Survival pushes us to look for answers to our spiritual questions and pain, and we start searching for alternative therapies that will provide healing and genuine wellbeing.

From the Arameans to the Amazonian cultures, Nazcas, Incas, Mayas, Aztecas, Han, Yorubas,

Druidas, Lakotas, Vedas, and more, all the ancient ancestral cultures hold a wonderful and magic legacy, safeguarded by our shamans, on the healing of the physical body, mind, emotions, astral body, and the soul, through the direct reconnection of the human soul with the spirits of the plants. This legacy teaches the art of holding the connection and equilibrium between the physical and the spiritual worlds, keeping and maintaining this connection always, using it to remember ourselves, our spiritual path, and the peace and love we shall bring into this world, teaching us to understand and join the evolutionary processes of life itself in a harmonious way.

An Ancient Lineage

I was born into such a shaman lineage in Peru. People in the town of Iquitos in the Amazon looked at us like we were weird. Neighbors sometimes made the sign of the cross in front of us like we were strange and dangerous people. But we had our own world and our own space and I did my best to ignore them.

My personal training started at a very young age, surrounded by women, a group of elders who always asked me to wake up early to go to our jungle parcel to pick the flowers and the aromatherapy plants for my mother to prepare the aromatherapy baths for her patients. Meanwhile, the women prepared the different plant medicines for each patient. They always asked me to pick the flowers or the leaves because when we are children, our energy is pure and strong. So when we pick them the energy of the plants keep their strong energy to heal. Of course, I had to be very careful because rattle snakes love to sleep at the bottom of the primroses.

After that we would have breakfast and I would go to school. Coming home, the house was always crowded with patients waiting for the important member of the women's group of healers to arrive so they could start working on healing them. I used to pass by them in my school uniform, saying "Good afternoon." They smiled because they saw just a normal little child. But then I would go get changed into my white working clothes and come back to the group. They were always so surprised, their faces plainly saying, "Uh, is this little child the important spiritual member we are waiting for to start?"

It was not always a fun life for a strange child who had a special gift. I'd always seen the spirits—something watching me, observing me in the dark like a black shadow sometimes—and I didn't understand what it was. I used to feel things and I was always scared. My mother tried to explain. But when you're a child you don't understand very well. Sometimes my parents would give me a drop or two of Ayahusaca before bed in order to have a good night's sleep under the protection of the plant spirit.

By age seven or eight I was drinking special teas and learning about the medicines. Shamanism is a very serious path, requiring many years of dedication to spiritual training. This is a path of life at the service of the community with the first years of training consisting of various chapters of apprenticeship, including isolation in the Amazon Rainforest with an elder shaman (normally a family member), learning to recognize every plant in situ in the forest and connect with their spirits and work with them. When you're in the jungle working with the plants you just see the plants like a lot of people hanging around, except all of the "people" are the spirits of the plants.

Training includes the drinking of all those plants or using them as aromatherapy baths.

Initiation consists of nine years of learning. Depending on the plant, every diet runs for nine days to nine weeks to nine months, up to nine years, learning the medicinal benefits of the plants, and also their magical powers. At the end of drinking a particular plant diet, the apprentice must participate in a special Ayahuasca ceremony to center the energy power of the diet plant and especially to connect with the spirit of the plant.

Some plants are very strong so you can only drink them for like nine days or maybe three. Other plants you cook them and make an extract and that extract you need to drink for up to 90 days. Sometimes, when you do a decoction, you go into the jungle and you drink this diet for at least 30 days just having plantain and the plant. Then you come off the diet for one week, take a rest, and then once again you go back to your place in the jungle with another plant.

I remember I was doing aromatherapy baths with Catawa, which is a poisonous plant. A single drop of this plant and you can die. But we use the Catawa bath for protection and I was able to see the spirit of this plant. It was like a monkey, a black monkey with red eyes. It was really scary with this monkey coming for nine days to look at me, alone in my little hut in the jungle, trying to see if I was afraid of him. I had to tell him, "I'm not afraid of you!" But I was practically shitting my pants. I was only 17.

At times I couldn't help thinking, *What am I doing*

here when all my friends from school are out having fun, going to the disco, drinking tequila, and falling in love while I'm out here alone, shitting and puking plant medicines in the jungle?

One time I was on a diet, feeling bored always drinking and talking with the spirits of the plants. I was with my Yabu Yaba (shaman grandmother and teacher) at the time, walking through the jungle when she says, "You are dreaming of your city life while the spirit of the medicine is walking on top of your feet."

I stopped my thoughts and felt something cold passing over the top of my feet. I froze and stood still like a statue as an Aguaje Machaco snake (Rusty Whipsnake) passed on top of me. Fortunately, she seemed not to have any interest in biting me. She just passed on top of my feet to remind me that there is danger everywhere we go if we are not paying attention!

As a teenager, I became rebellious and decided to challenge myself and choose the most difficult path possible, the Brave Men Shaman Path—to be an Ayahuasca Death Dancer. Normally a path only for brave men and some elder women chosen by destiny, people tried to tell me, "Oh, no, you don't want to do that, not a young girl like you." But I thought, *What is the point of being able to see and work with the spirits and not use the gift in the most powerful way possible to help people?*

I decided I could be as brave as any man and show the rest of my people that this path is not only for men. We women can go on this path, too, seducing the spirits of death better than a man!

Dancing with the Death Angels

Ayahuasca is a sacred plant. By connecting with her, you take part in the awakening of the third eye to the CosmoVision, the inner and universal Magico-Spiritual world. All that we cannot see with our normal eyes, we can experience with our third eye and intuition.

Many Amazon shamans consider Ayahuasca as the means of universal training, accessing not only the spirits of plants from the jungle but plants from all over the world as well. Ayahuasca also enables us to see past, present and future as well as the evolution of humanity. After the first five years of training come the open Ayahuasca ceremonies with patients where the shaman elder teaches the apprentices how to heal and treat each patient. For nine years we learn how to perform a ceremony and how to diagnose a sick person on the physical and spiritual planes. The shamans normally work all together in groups and families to teach the new apprentices different ways of healing.

And then there is learning how to dance with the Angels of Death. It is all energetic. It's not about words. The art of getting connected is more like dancing. You have to know how to approach the angels, how to get close, how to make a connection. You cannot just face them, boom, like that.

Terminally ill people come to the jungle either to die or to live. That's it. My Yabu Yaba had a technique and I would bring her extreme cases. We'd drink the medicine and she'd say, "Okay, can you realize their Angel of Death? Can you see where it is? Can you see what it is? Is it in front? Is it sitting inside the person?" She worked with me to establish communication, to learn how long a person had left by reading the position and posture and actions of their Angel of Death. And then would come the negotiation process on behalf of the patient. Sometimes it would almost be like a fight, a conflict of power, standing there for the patient saying basically "Gimme a break!"

I recall a Japanese woman the doctors had declared terminal with bone cancer. One shaman had already sent her away because she was so sick he was afraid she would die in his camp and get him in trouble. She had been suffering high fevers every night for six years and was so skinny, bony, and pale. Nothing could stop those fevers.

I took her to the camp of my Yabu Yaba. It was the middle of the night when we got there, but, of course, she was expecting us. The woman was too weak to drink with us in the first Ayahuasca ceremony. My grandmother asked if I could see her death angel and I could. He was a strange looking monk, completely dark, with robes, and he was sitting just behind her. My grandmother was singing as I tried to get closer to him, and I was singing with her. The patient was laying down and the death angel was noninvasive—not inside of her body—he was just taking care of her, watching her, nothing else. When I approached, he moved away a little bit but was able to connect with me. It felt like he was giving me space to work and he was enjoying the singing, feeling it, accepting our presence with her.

"If he is not inside her and she is not inside him and he's just observing her from the right side it means she's not dying," grandmother said. "She still has time."

The Japanese woman turned out to be a Buddhist, which is why I saw the Buddhist monk Angel of Death. After a week of plant medicines her fever broke. After that we started giving her plants to center her body and to center her spirit in her body. Soon she could join us in the Ayahuasca ceremonies. Over time, she learned the plants and learned how to create her own medicines. When she finally came out of the jungle a year later and called her family, they were so surprised. They'd long ago held a funeral for her and her husband had remarried!

There are different kinds of Angels of Death and not every shaman can see them. There is a moment when you see their eyes, like shining lights. Some have eyes like bowls of light. The angels themselves vary according to the patient's origins and bloodline. The Angels of Death for the British people and the Irish are usually Druids, for example. The spirits of the Druids are so nice and they have the most gorgeous faces. You can just about fall in love with them!

One scientist that came from America had brain cancer. He was obviously Caucasian, but when we started with the ceremonies his Angel of Death turned out to be a Native American Apache. A huge native man, this Angel of Death was always on the patient's back, sitting there and getting inside his body. He would start chanting with us in his own tongue whenever my grandmother and I would approach doing our chants. He was very impressive. The scientist came to work with us once a year for five years until he finally stopped coming.

Cultural Amalgamation

Today, there are new technologies with very

advanced practices to treat diseases with strong chemicals and drugs that most of the time just kill the pain but don't heal the diseases. This is the reason why more and more people are on the search for alternative methods—so much so that we are now living in the new era fusing modern medicine with ancestral traditions from different cultures, treating diseases with much more success than before, with better applications into the actual problems besetting us.

The use of Ayahuasca as a method of therapy has recently become widespread around the world because of the plant's multiple applications at every level of psychological work—human behavior, group therapy, inspirational work and more. What was once the extremely forbidden and occult Ayahuasca Death Dance—a ritual only practiced in extreme cases of imminent terminal disease— is now an eagerly sought-after experience by people suffering from the many physical, mental, emotional, psychic, and spiritual illnesses brought about by living in modern Western society.

This is a very good thing. But, as a traditionally-trained shaman, I see that there are many pitfalls and things that people need to watch out for. When I am asked to read research papers and books by cultural anthropologists and scientists, I find many mistakes. It is one thing to go into a community and live for three months, taking notes for a book. It is another thing to live in that community for ten years or a lifetime. Not only do the shamans not give the whole story to researchers, they cannot. Working with the plants is not an intellectual thing. That is the smallest part of the medicine.

If you haven't done at least a minimum of nine

years basic training in the jungle, please keep away from doing this type of work. Many diseases can be transmitted energetically or in a spiritual way. Instead of healing your patient you will end up getting sick with the same diseases as your patient. In our Amazonian culture this is well known as the "Law of the Cutipa," which consists of the exchange or transference of the dark energies from the sick person to the healer.

During my life work, I have seen many healers from all over the world coming into the jungle to receive treatment for the same illnesses they got from their patients. Many psychotherapists come with the same depression as their patients, the same burnout, the same psychotic crisis. Same thing with very young healers who do a fast few months at some healing school learning things like Reiki or massage therapy. Very soon they are told they are ready to work with the energy of other people. So they start doing it and after a couple of years they start feeling and showing the same symptoms as their former patients.

For example, "Mary" was a European woman who did a short-time basic apprentice study to become a healer in one of the hundreds of healing schools all over Europe. She started working with a woman with breast cancer. After a year of treating her favorite breast cancer patient, her patient got much better and left the therapy. But a couple of months later Mary woke up to the horrible nightmare of developing breast cancer herself.

After breast tissue removal, radiotherapy and chemotherapy, the medical establishment told her there was nothing else to do for her. So, she came into the far Amazon rain forest. But, as with most of the terminal patients that come, she arrived only in time to go on her spiritual death-quest work to find the courage to be able to accept death as another level of life.

If you are learning to do even simple healing work, it is very important to learn all the protocols of working with energy. These protocols must include learning detox diets with plants and aromatherapy baths with the proper plants for a minimum of five years. Only in this way can you learn their individual energies and know and become known by their spirits. And remember, if you work with patients every day, it is very important to go on a special detox with plants to cleanse at least once a year as a preventive way of eliminating all the dark energy from the diseases of your patients.

If you are working with plants, doing therapies, the most important thing is you need to learn how to prepare your own plant medicines. The plants themselves will absorb your energy. When I go visit shamans the first thing I ask is, "Do you cook your medicine or did you buy it from somebody else?" If they say, "No, I'm buying it from some elder shaman," well, this person is not a shaman at all. No shaman would drink medicine that is from someone else. You have to cook your medicine so it is of your own energy, otherwise it doesn't work properly. It can't become your ally. This is so logical and so basic it always shocks me when I find healers who don't know this.

It is also important to learn how to help patients to interpret their Ayahuasca CosmoVisions. Every CosmoVision is unique, with a deep spiritual message enclosed within every picture or scene that you experience during the ritual. This is a very private and personal experience about your direct connection with the cosmic universe, your reconnection with your God, with the Mother Earth, in a private space nobody can penetrate, not even the shaman.

Sometimes during the encounter with Ayahuasca, people cannot visualize anything. But messages come in different ways. "Liza," a sweet housewife suffering from chronic dermic psoriasis, had tried hundreds of treatments with no success. She visited an old shaman lady for healing with Ayahuasca. She had no visions, just darkness and silence, except for the noise of hundreds of bees flying around her. The next day she went back home sad, thinking Ayahuasca had no message for her.

A few months later she attended one of my lectures and told me about her frustrating experience. I smiled and said, "Sometimes she won't show pictures. This way you will have to focus on just one thing. In your case, it's the bees. Research natural bee-based medicines." Two weeks later she called to say she was working with a medicine made of bee venom. In this way she started her healing process.

Sometimes the Ayahuasca CosmoVisions can introduce you into her secret, mystical, mythological iconography, bringing a deep spiritual message for you. "Jessie," a young secretary, saw herself in the middle of the jungle surrounded by old big trees. Suddenly an old being came out of a tree holding a ceramic bowl. "Drink the medicine of my house," he said, pointing to the tree. "With this medicine you will be able to heal your soul." She drank and millions of green leaves grew all over her body, wrapping her in a green cocoon of leaves. Then she transformed into a huge blue morpho butterfly, opened her wings, and started flying.

When asked about it, I explained that the soul is like a mirror. Sometimes this mirror breaks into pieces. This normally happens in the moment of death. But it can also break when a child is the victim of abuse, causing many problems later in life. I said, "The old man was giving you a plant to heal your fragmented soul. But you will also need to go on a plant detox diet to continue with this healing. Ayahuasca already showed you the way and the plant to use."

Sometimes you go into re-experiencing the most impressive bad or good moments of your life, seeing and tasting once again all that caused you so much pain. This way you can face the traumas from a very different perspective, awakening all those enclosed emotions, clearing them up so you can heal yourself from the traumas you were carrying in your unconscious memory. We can also go into a future experience where we can see ourselves some years ahead and see how our lives will be. This is also very healing because this way we do not need to waste our time on worries for the future and can focus on the most important processes we are in at that moment.

As you can see, Ayahuasca is a plant with great intelligence that works in a very deep way inside our mind, psyche, and body—but especially our souls—healing every aspect of us. She helps us to clear our minds from all the garbage and psychic attacks we receive every moment of every day into our brains—advertisements, fake news, all the toxic manipulative people sending stuff towards us—all this garbage gets cleared in such a way that we can rebuild ourselves based on our own wishes and goals for the future without any type of influence.

The moment you get to understand that everything in life is part of an order in the universe and that the universe is inside *you*—this is the moment where you understand that you don't need to look outside to others for anything. This is the moment you see how wonderful your own body is and how it shines inside. And that is when you realize that nothing is more important than you healing yourself.

The Gift

Every plant has its own elemental or spirit, the same as the ocean, rivers, lakes, mountains and all that is in nature. These spirits have various shapes and forms. Some of the representations are ancient, some of them are new. The most rare shapes are those that mix human and animal shapes, according to where they originated in ancient ancestral times—for example, from Lemuria, or Atlantis, or sometimes from other worlds. When they are represented in an iconographic way by nature, sometimes we can recognize them.

Here are two drawings of a few elementals that shamans frequently work with in the Amazon.

Yacuruna (Waterhealer)

The Yacuruna is one of the most important deities of the Amazon Rainforest, very feared and respected by the shamans and Amazon ethnic communities. (For a powerful depiction, see the movie *The Shape of Water*.) Also known as the Watergod or Waterhealer, a powerful Yacuruna is always described riding a huge black alligator with a live black boa at his waist as a belt. Most River Shamans performing an Ayahuasca ritual invoke the magic spirit of the Yacurunas to come help heal their patients or come teach their children about water medicine energy. The Yacurunas have their temporary houses at the bottom of the Renaco trees. According to the elder Amazon shamans, there are hidden interdimensional doors inside the Amazon River that, when you spirit journey with

Ayahuasca and go deep into the Amazon River, you can find the doors and enter Atlantis. There you may encounter the very wise ancient elder masters

of Atlantis who teach the River Shamans powerful magical ways of healing.

El Chullachaquis O Kasppirunas

A very wide variety of Tree Spirits, Chullachaqui or KasppiRunas (people from the trees) are the caretakers or spiritual guardians of the trees of the Amazon Rainforest and the rest of the world. They are the ones who keep the knowledge of the medicinal uses of the plants and they help us to reconnect to the plant spirits. Some of them are caretakers of the animals, snakes, birds, and insects. The Shapingos, little young spirits of the bushes, love to play and confuse people until they get lost in the jungle. Normally this happens when they want to heal or teach the person about strength and intuition. The elders spirits usually help the shamans by teaching them how to use the leaves of the plants or just the energy of a tree to heal a person.

CHAPTER 2

Alan Leon received his "higher education" in the Northern Rocky Mountains, camping, usually alone, for 18 years, eventually including the Sonoran and Mojave deserts in his explorations. He spent the 80s guiding horseback camping trips near Glacier Park, Montana. In 1991, he worked as a hiking/camping guide in Sedona, Arizona. An accepted friend at the kitchen tables of many Native American homes, he has been blessed to have many traditional family elders guiding his way. In 1992 he traveled to Peru and Bolivia. For 20 years he lived in remote village homes, absorbing the healing ways of many tribes. In 1993 he organized spiritual tourism centered around traditional healers in twelve locations and various cultures in Peru. In 2002 he was initiated into the Kallawaya lineage high in the Andes above Lake Titicaca in the area of Charazani, Boliva. Alan continues to guide in Peru for a few weeks a year, and his shamanic guiding has evolved, in a natural way, into hospice work, caring for the dying. But he mostly wanders and camps the western wilds, praying in the old ways with a beloved Mother Bear Spirit.

He can be reached at http://www.conscioushospice.com & https://www.consciouscamping.net

Dead Shamans and Changing Times

It is a winter's dark new moon night in the Sonoran desert, somewhat south of a place named Nothing, Arizona. As usual, around midnight, I wake to walk dark under the stars. This night I walk, wondering how to tell this tale.

The old shamans that we knew have all died—died without leaving any apprentices attaining the depth and the extraordinary mastery in the healing ways the villagers in Peru and Bolivia have learned to expect of them for the past several thousand years.

I walk in the dark, musing on how the last of the ancient lineage healers I worked with high in the Andes above Lake Titicaca—the Kallawayas near Charazani, Boliva, descendants of the ancient civilization of Tiwanacu who built in megalithic glory more than ten thousand years ago—have all left their bodies some ten years past. Though, as a visceral fact, at times they continue to visit with me. So, you could say we've been together for well over twenty years now.

But then yesterday, climbing the hills through tall cactus stands of Saguaro, I realized the last two hospice deaths I attended had been without my teachers hovering about, holding my hand. Could be the time has come to let loose and fly.

Harsh Roots

I was born into the church of my hellfire-and-damnation preacher father, receiving my first life imprinting in that white Republican Christian community. I was taught the rest of the world is wrong and going to hell—raised to fear that if I made one wrong step outside the many church rules that an angry god would burn me forever in the same hell the rest of the world deserved.

Entering school, I found my friends—people I readily liked—among those that the church called the damned. And, in accordance with Bible instruction to not spoil the child by sparing the rod, I got belt beatings for spending too much time with these non-church children, creating a painful confusion around the concept of a "loving god," my father, and how to interact with the world at large. Though by grace and thank good Goddess, eventually nature had her way with me, awakening a core true self. At a very young age I began leaving the house and climbing the mountains near Pasadena, California.

Through my youth, in the many places we lived, I carried on with my outdoors adventures. The forest and rivers taught me there is a world of miraculous rightness, beauty and grace. As a result of this discovery, I grew independent in my teens and rejected the church. And so, too, the people of the church rejected me, leaving me with a deep core belief that I am a social reject and god-damned and that pretty much everybody and everything agrees that I just shouldn't exist.

It's hard to carry on with anything like a normal life being so crippled inside. After high school I went to live deep in the Northern Rockies, usually alone, remaining in the wilderness months at a time, setting a course that remains my way today.

One Rocky Mountain night, my frustration with the god I was taught of came to a head. Climbing a hill, I shook my fists to the sky yelling, "Alright, if you are real let me know now or just fuck you forever!" I raged, ranted and cried through the night. Then, at daybreak, totally unexpected, from behind Spirit Mother slipped her loving arms around me, giving a completely physical touch with that magnetic agreement that flows through the emotional core—that feeling we call love. Even today, with tears in my eyes, I tell you this is the clearest experience I've yet felt in this life.

In time, this loving relationship with this feminine spirit I call Grandmother opened me to receiving full support from true masculinity, or Grandfather. I won't even begin guessing our origins, roles or final forms. It's sufficient to feel kinship and acceptance, and in this current realm of consciousness I am grateful to have the approachable experience of loving grandparents in spirit. With them I celebrate each day, along with a great community of spirit family I came to see and interact with in the wild lands.

Thus, when I arrived in the Andes and Amazon, the people there recognized me as also one of nature's children. Having suffered centuries of abuse at the hands of the church, our wounds recognized each other. They utterly took me in.

Given the trueness of spirit that has come to guide and live through me, I am now vastly grateful that the normal life was not available to me.

The Kallawaya

When first I began regularly visiting the Kallawayas (shamans) in the Andes, the only regular public transportation that would climb into the mountains of their villages were open-back farm trucks. I would just wave down a ride from any truck heading in the right direction.

The large truck beds would fill with local produce, usually potatoes, wool, and charky (alpaca jerky), and the people and their personal belongings would top the pile. The journey from La Paz to Charazani, the main town of the Kallawaya area, could take a couple days—if all went well. However, the tires were often old and there were many flats to be changed. Rains often brought mudslides and we'd have to clear the debris away. Sometimes the road would wash out, leaving holes that dropped off the mountain. Precarious temporary bridges would be built of stacked stones just wide enough for the truck tires to be narrowly supported above some steep mountain abyss. One of the few things we didn't suffer was boredom.

One time I made the Charazani journey and then beyond to the home of the Kallawaya Juan de Dios. As I walked up, the door opened and Juan pulled me in. The offering was laid out and ready to go. He had already seen what was troubling me in a dream and knew exactly when I would arrive. That magician was well plugged in.

It took six years of visiting with them before the Kallawayas, Papa Pablo and Tio Pinto (like saying dad and uncle), began telling me the mountain spirits were saying I could be initiated into the lineage. Through the ages past, most often it had been those born gifted with strong spirit connections who would be noticed during childhood, and a natural bond would develop with the current healing master. The student would accompany the healer for decades—twenty to forty years of apprenticeship was possible.

Then would come a strong sign. Most of the

healers I lived with were struck by lightning. One of our family's grandfathers was struck three times in the heart. A blue light came down off the mountain and entered a woman we worked with by Lake Titicaca. The first shaman I met of my lineage purposefully shook my hand with a lightning-twisted arm.

After all that, the aspiring healer would still have to gain village approval. True healings would have to happen for them to prove themselves. A charlatan was not going to pull anything over on the experienced village elders, or likely anyone else within the collective of tribal tradition. Nor were inflated egos tolerated.

For years I declined and delayed. I didn't feel worthy or capable of sharing the lineage. My Christian-based core wound still insisted I shouldn't even exist. "I'm gringo," I protested, "a wanderer, not one of the native villagers." But the Kallawayas and spirits were insistent.

The last time I questioned the calling, I stood alone on a mountain ridge. Then a condor came. She circled me three times at eye level, just a few meters away, so close as to make point-driven eye contact. The last time around she opened her beak wide in a silent scream, wind-whipped feathers whistling.

In tears I cried, "Come on, Alan, wake up!"

Eventually and hesitatingly, I agreed to the initiation. Papa Pablo took me to Cota Cota, a ceremony site in the mountains used for thousands of years, and had me create the offering. Cota means lake in the ancient language of Aymara. Papa Pablo told me that long ago it was a village with lakes on both sides. It now lies in ruins on a knife-edged mountain ridge, high and dry. What cataclysms so changed the land? How many millennia had the magicians been coming here to pray in this place?

Meanwhile, Papa Pablo, in deep communion with a large clan gathering of spirits, received unanimous agreement to my initiation. The old lineage was placed in me. Not long after that, Papa Pablo and Tio Pinto, the last of the healer Kallawayas we knew of died. Though our families searched the area for more healers, none were then found.

The Old Ways

The old ones capable of profound healing were quiet and honestly humble. Most of them weren't to be called any special honoring name, such as Don or Dona so-and-so. A Shipibo shaman I visited for many years we called Carlitos, in sweet endearment. Maria at Lake Titicaca was simply Maria. My main teacher of the Kallawayas I came to lovingly call Papa Pablo.

These beloved shamans joyfully showed me very much the opposite of Christian condemnation. (Good goddess, I love those folks with my life.) You can imagine how deeply touched I was to find sweetly humble teachers in gentle spirituality. There is plenty enough pain to go around in this life simply from existing. No need to add it to our spirit connection.

Visiting the Andean shamans usually took a few days of high-altitude trekking to ancient family compounds. The people there were wearing mostly the homespun wool of their alpacas, the men in thick and durable white wool pants, the women in many layers of thick brown wool skirts that they have brightly hemmed. All wore sandals made of used tire rubber, no matter how cold it got.

When brought to the high peaks near Machu Picchu to meet my first Andean grandfather, Abuelo Sinchi, an altomsayoc (a high healer), as usual we piled together on the floor for the night. (Their traditional low-walled homes are built of stacked stone with mud chinking in some, but not all, of the gaps between the rocks. The roofs are piled thick with yellowed grass making the homes look like livable haystacks.) Just before daybreak the family and I shared a dream in which we were seated around Grandfather as he instructed us. Then we all awoke at the same moment with Grandfather saying that I am one of them, one of the family. Grandfather then went to the door and greeted our Divine Mother and Father and the mountain spirits and then each of us. So commenced a ceremonial party that lasted all day and well into the night, celebrating our newfound relation.

Coca leaf is a prayer way to connect with Pachamama (Earth Mother). Typically Andean healers will pray with coca leaves, casting (gently dropping) them to fall in various patterns, the falling leaves overlapping or forming a cross, touching or separate, greenside or pale-side up, odd leaf shapes and more are the "letters" of leaf reading. When I first met the Q'ero shamans near Cusco, they decided on a coca casting ceremony to check me out. When the leaves were cast from the Q'ero shaman's hand, quite improbably they all fell together in a straight line, positive sides showing up. Both shamans showed surprise. Quickly the leaves were gathered up and cast again. And again the leaves fell straight line positive sides. The Q'eros, a bit shocked, then told me they needed to take me to meet the old man of the mountain, Old Mariano, who lived in the peaks of Ausangate, the highest and most powerful mountain above Cusco.

Mariano was also an altomsayoc, among the highest capacity of Andean healers. On that first visit he told me I always was welcome and please return. Upon returning, he gifted me his coca bag.

During the use of coca leaves, experienced healers are triggered by the leaves and, at times, will psychically read astonishingly detailed and insightful nuances of a patient's life. Healers will be instructed as to where there are imbalances and perhaps their sources. When the spirit-informed diagnosis is understood, a focusing ceremonial offering is made, enabling the energy-pattern changes to be made.

Andean offerings are usually small plates on which we piled the goodies to be given. Among the Kallawaya we used flat sea shells. A nest of cotton formed the base, then came coca leaves we had prayed with. Over this came various foods, flowers and other small items corresponding to the things of our life that we were showing gratitude for. During the creation of the offering a magic of material and spirit correspondence is being built. Traditionally corn beer was offered. (Nowadays wine or other alcohol is sprinkled or poured as offering.) Each healer had their various ways and items to be given. At the end of the ceremony the nests were burned in offering to Mother. All along there was much prayer and communion.

One time, a friend of mine came to see the Kallawaya Juan de Dios. My friend was using a prescribed blood thinner that had side effects and that would, in time, kill him. The ceremonial offering was performed, and when my friend got home his two doctors were surprised to see him healed and they took him off the medicine. I witnessed many physical ailments cured that modern medicine hadn't been able to affect, experiencing the shamans' ability to see into problems of the psyche blocking life-giving flows of love in relationships, learning, work, finances, home and such. Through arrangements in spirit, the blocked negative patterns were changed to the positive ways again.

Along with Divine Mother and Father there is an extended spirit family we work with. Ancestors, animal and plant guides, consciousness of landscapes and sites, nature spirits. Ancient cultures around the world have always known them. Like caring elder siblings they are really quite capable and willing to be of help. Though their powers can induce awe, we don't worship them. But we sure do love them. They can be really good friends and we get together often. To actually connect and fluently converse with this spirit family was the ability of the shamans that were truly healers.

Woven through these decades with the Kallawaya were also nearly twenty years visiting various shamans in the Peruvian Amazon rainforest. Experiences with their Ayahuasca formulas continue to open wondrous inner and inter-dimensional inspirations. With the Shipibo tribes in the Amazon the spirit connection was usually made during Ayahuasca ceremony, with psychic/spirit spontaneity directing inter-dimensional singing.

Song-sound moves fantastic flows—triggering feeling/visual experiences into the dimensions beyond our normal band of sense receptivity. The singing, along with the plant powers, re-patterns both body and psyche of those who come for healing.

At times Mama Ayahuasca would call me and I would get up and walk off into the jungle. The shamans, in deep connection and wisdom, would smile and say, "There he goes again." I could not see trees nor trail. What I saw was the exquisite energy patterns of life, perfectly interfaced through all, the trees, me, and everything. I would be walked through the forest in easy agreement. At times I would get in my tiny log dugout canoe and paddle into strong-current rivers, paddling through the patterns in stupendous harmony.

The shamans were sure of the healing outcomes of their ceremonies. Part of their honest humility was in knowing that the life-changing help and healing came through our spirit family and that life itself was making the necessary energy-pattern rearrangements that would work so well for the people in need of help and healing.

The ceremonies themselves were fairly informal. Dogs ran through, children piping in. Participants could move about. At times we were encouraged to talk and laugh, celebrating our blessings. The Ese-Eha of the Tambopata River told us that their grandparents talked of the long-ago days when the ceremonies were a party-like celebration.

Ah, the good old days. Obviously this approach was more widespread before the Catholic church brought them the idea that you have to suffer to be spiritual.

Times of Change

Juan de Dios died right after my last visit. And yet his family continued to see him with me. At times I still feel him hold my hand and he sometimes speaks. Some years previous, Grandfather Shinchi, in solstice prayers, performed a ceremony of sharing with me his heart. As I was leaving, he cried, and he died very soon after.

Old Mariano warned me just before he died to not carry on in ceremony with some of the inflated egos that would follow his departure. Sure enough, not long after he died there were those going around charging big money for ceremonies but not healing anybody. Now, from the connected web of the many villages of my families and the many more villages of their contacts, I hear the people reporting that there are no healers among them that have risen through the traditional time-taking, exacting process. None have the high spirit connection and the depth of life-changing healing as those before, so there is no one that the villagers will go to for healing.

This is not to say that I know how it is everywhere else. But this is the report I've been getting from the simple earth people, indigenous to their culture and place, who are looking to find true healers to help them again.

For the last six years I've returned to my wilderness wandering ways in North America, allowing the rightness of the lands to have their way with this nature's child, connecting, feeling, loving, with Grandmother connecting through earth, Grandfather opening to sky, joining in prayer with the many spirits of the lands, sharing travels with a beloved Medicine Bear Bundle, some of the items within it which have been prayed with for over 5,000 years. I migrate, camping the Western wilds from the southern Sonoran deserts to Montana's northern Rockies, enjoying the time to pray the old ways in these vast lands.

Twice I have experienced near death. The first time, dropping mysteriously ill in the mountains, aching and groaning a death song until I noted my heart and breathing had stopped. I woke in the morning to a peace that passes understanding. The second time, having trained in deep yogic breathing for some years, practicing at my teacher's altar, I seemingly stopped breathing and was in stillness for two hours—relaxed and comfortable while time was experienced as just a moment.

Both experiences resulted in wondrous clarity, peace and loving. Now, with all this stripping away, it has been a natural thing to go with the calling to attend to the dying. Now I can be present in depth understanding during people's uncomfortable, dark-hard moments that can be a part of dying, as well as the glory and some deeply worthy shamanic sharing. My Kallawaya teachers often show up and at times the spirit family of the one dying will get together with my spirit family and the death room will fill with stupendous great grace. I am still available for such work and am called on at times. Being well practiced in crawling through my own dark has made me a knowledgeable and compassionate companion as I meet folks in their various hard times.

The Gift

I walk in the desert dark, musing on how the last

of the ancient lineage healers I worked with have passed—how their depth connection and their humbleness within awesome healing capacities have passed with them. The environments and forces that created the ancient tribes are not the same as today's. As a source of sanity, some ancient ways may remain the same a while longer. I carry these inside me and share them with those who are open. But clinging past a healthy ending to what is no more can devolve into mere fetish worship.

Some of us within the shamanic world have already grieved for the old that has died while at the same time growing in our confidence in miraculous life and spirit bringing the next ways. To be the new growth we must step beyond our history. Some of us have begun experiencing the time for the ending of much that was previous to make way for new beginnings.

Perhaps nature herself is forming the next beginnings?

Whew! That's a thought. Just when we appear to be at the edge of global cataclysmic climate change. Ah, just now, while writing this, five vultures arrived in the near sky with some sort of agreement.

Through ages past it has been the shaman's role to warn and guide those that would listen. There are many old-culture histories of those that survived following the spirit guides.

My deep immersion in the natural world has opened me to eco-grief, and waves of feeling sometimes wash over me as I stand with Earth and cry. There is an enormity of killing and suffering happening throughout Earth's many creatures. She has lost 50 percent of her wildlife in just the last 40 years. Since 1970 there is 50 percent less life in the seas. We are tumbling into the next mass extinction ... an enormous event most people don't yet feel.

There is a mounting collective feeling of future fear in the face of upcoming, life-threatening, extreme weather changes. Now is a good time to deepen our connection with our sustaining Earth, to better move with her when she goes to whatever next will be. Humanity evolves, matures, and if we survive there is a great potential of expanding into a glorious global unity.

If there is anything I can share with you, good reader, if you find it true to you, and that is to seek conscious communion with nature. It can be an excellent way to the true self—perhaps not the "you" your childhood culture and upbringing would demand, not the "you" hiding behind defenses built of pain, but rather the being you are as Life tells the story, loving right here, right now, naturally.

Ask ... and listen ...

Prayer is like visiting home, with many an "I love you too." Grandmother has me sit beside her in a feeling of equality. All of our beloved buddies, the spirits of the lands, are so willing to help, to be here for us—not at all like desperately beseeching some god way out there.

Prayer can be simply saying hello and feeling into the greater picture. Seldom do I ask anything. But when I do ask for directions, it is clear that the consciousness replying is different than my normal ego voices, with answers different to or beyond what I may have thought.

I hope for you, dear reader, such visceral/spirit experience.

CHAPTER 3

Simon Buxton is Founder/Director of The Sacred Trust and has worked and trained within shamanic traditions for over three decades. For fifteen years he served as a faculty member of Dr. Michael Harner's The Foundation For Shamanic Studies, and also undertook a formal thirteen year apprenticeship, as detailed within his book *The Shamanic Way of the Bee* which was the recipient of the Canizares Book Award for non-fiction. He is the co-author of *Darkness Visible*, and his next two books are in preparation. Simon is an elected Fellow of The Royal Anthropological Institute, the world's longest-established scholarly association dedicated to the furtherance of anthropology and he is a life member of the Oxford University Anthropological Society. His work has been profiled within several books including *Travelling Between the Worlds* and *Soul Companions* as well as being featured in the documentary film *Vanishing of the Bees*. In 2007, as part of the ongoing development of The Sacred Trust, Simon Buxton and his partner Naomi Lewis opened the only residential teaching center in the UK dedicated to the study of shamanism. It is here that they live with their son and conduct their writing, research and teaching work.

He can be reached at https://sacredtrust.org/

A New Pearl of Great Price: Shamanism, Darkness and the Path of Pollen

It was in the spring of 1982, a couple of years after writing his seminal work *The Way of the Shaman*, that the cultural anthropologist, shaman and valued mentor in my own work, Michael Harner, sought to undertake a power quest in a cave in the Shenandoah Valley of Virginia. He quickly discovered that the darkness of the cave was "thick and silent," and surrounded by this dense darkness he went on to have a series of remarkably potent and transformative experiences.

But what role—if any—did the physical darkness itself play in his supernatural encounters within the cave? It is well recognized that animism forms the milieu of shamanism or, put another way we might simply state that *everything that is, is alive*. This clearly supposes that it is not only the visible natural world that lives; the trees, the bees, the caves, clouds and rivers, but that darkness itself is alive and animated with spirit. In other words, through the shaman's eyes, darkness is far from being merely the absence of light (as a modern Westerner might typically describe it). Rather it is understood and engaged with as living spirit. Beyond that, within a number of indigenous and native cultures, this living darkness is known to be the most ancient spirit in the universe; the first-mother, she who gave birth to all of life including the deities of every pantheon of light. This is certainly the case within the tradition in which I was to train, a living vibrant European shamanic tradition that works with the honeybee and the hive as its central, sentient motif.

Four years and a handful of months after Michael's

work in the cave I was to have my own encounter with the living darkness within the ritualized context of this European shamanic tradition that in the modern world is known as the Path of Pollen and in days of yore was referred to as the Forest Way. The fuller details of this encounter lie elsewhere (see *The Shamanic Way of the Bee*) but suffice to say, spending 23 days and nights uninterrupted within a specially constructed, large blacked-out hexagonal basket brought about a crossing of the Rubicon that realigned the trajectory of my life forever more.

The basket itself is formally known as the *oneiricell*. This is a composite of the words *oneiric* and *cell*, the former relating to the Greek term for dreams and dreaming, the latter referencing the six-sided waxen compartment into which the honeybee egg is placed. What follows is gestation. The egg becomes first the larva, then the pupa and, if a male drone, emerges as a fully formed bee child on its 24th day having spent the previous 23 days and nights in the protected darkness of the cell within the protected darkness of the hive. This oneiricell was initially introduced to me by a term that I falsely took to be rather more prosaic and humdrum, namely "the clam." Little did I comprehend at that time that here was a power object par excellence, which, in fact, was perfectly so named after this two-shelled mollusk. For like the proverbial grain of sand which over an extended period may become the famed gemstone of the sea, so an alchemy might likewise occur within and upon the apprentice who had been placed within it, emerging in eventuality a human transformed: *the new pearl of great price*. (A term coined by the late medieval alchemist Petrus Bonus.)

Having been placed within the clam following a

harrowing experience of being stung in multiplicity by honeybees on specifically targeted areas of my body so as to bring about a particular condition of visioning and vulnerability, I became a witness to myself for what felt to be endless days and nights of torturous inner struggle and turmoil, including periods of crippling fears and unmitigated terrors. Curiously perhaps, these fears and terrors were never of the darkness itself but rather catalyzed by the presence of the thick and heavy mantle of truth that the darkness lay upon me. For it was my own thoughts and the thoughts behind those thoughts that I feared and which seemed to be creating a rough and narrow furrow that was leading me but to one final destination: the asylum.

What eventually saved me from losing my battle with and for my mind was a single word — *surrender* — uttered to me with a honed and forceful precision at my moment of greatest vulnerability. And it was that word alone, thrown out to me as a lifeline by my beloved teacher, which allowed me to grasp but the thinnest of golden threads that lead to my truer golden self, ensuring that forever drowning in a stygian labyrinthine night was not to be my fate. On hearing that word and receiving it as a command from superior officer to foot soldier, I acquiesced to the injunction. In so doing, the mind was finally able to settle downwards towards the heart and I was able to cease being a slave to my ego with its clumps and clusters of desperate, dissociated voices.

In the wake of this gradual settling, the darkness was then able to share herself as she has always done to those who traverse this shadow landscape: she came alive to my senses and commenced her dance. Over the uncounted hours and days that followed, she shape-shifted from one form to another; the cave of quiet of my mother's womb; a lover who curled her tenderness around me as I drifted into sleep; the slow-moving black serpent who weaved her way between dark and dark. With each moment that passed, and with every breath that I took, I allowed myself the ever more generous gift of surrender. I had arrived at a state that my teacher poetically described as being "both rooted to the Earth and anchored to the heavens."

Having finally arrived into this balanced suspended state between chthonic below and stellar above, I was then to be exposed to a variety of teachings within an environment that in the most natural of fashions encouraged extended periods of reflection and reverie. At what I had presumed was the dawn of each new day my teacher entered the room in which the oneiricell was housed and I was issued a *seed axiom* from the tradition. I was admonished to reflect, mull and meditate upon them, with the purpose of generating realizations and attaining understandings that would in turn allow me to make a slow and studied cortege upon this honeyed path. There are two seed axioms that are of particular relevance in the context of this essay, to wit:

1. Everything is born of woman

2. Matter is malleable

These axioms are relevant as they correspond directly to further revelations received that concern the very secret core of the bee tradition, issued in darkness "from mouth to ear." In preparation for and anticipation of receiving these arcane teachings, I was instructed to locate my awareness at my perineum. I had been aware that shamans in countless cultures recognized that communing with the spirits can occur most efficaciously at *thin* places, that is, locales where the distance between heaven and earth is perceived as negligible, such as crossroads or the area between where water and land come to meet. What took me by surprise was that the locus celebrated as the greatest example of such a thin place was to be found upon the human body at its very midpoint. "Between the up and the down, between the front and the back, between the right and the left. Between the place of urination and the place of defecation. This is where you must place your attention." Such was the instruction, and so began a practice that I was to adopt and, over time, become adept in, holding a focused concentration on what is considered to be a spirit road for ingress and egress of the ancestors and other tutelary ones.

The two primary bodies of teachings that I was exposed to in darkness and then elucidated over the following years were firstly the application of what is referred to as "The Impersonal Use of Sexual Energy." This vast body of work is based on the premise that the physical worlds—this matter of which we are all made—is amatory in nature, and that matter rejoices in matter. That every atom falls in love with other atoms and delights to make love with them to form both simple and complex structures that emerge as the outpouring of creativity, the most highly prized of human activities within this tradition.

The second body of work, intimately connected to the first, is the development and application of what are named *nektars*, this being the technical term for mundane fluids produced by the human body that have been transubstantiated via a corporeal alchemy into agents of healing and transformation known as *ichors*, fluids that were said to flow in the veins of the gods. As these fluids in their mundane form included urine, sweat, tears, menstrual blood, breast milk (produced by both men and women at will) and others that we are raised in modern Western culture to consider have no value and are to be rejected and discarded, I initially found myself nose-to-nose with my own prejudices about how I felt on receiving these revelations and on being asked to imbibe these apparently holy fluids! The praxes (practice) involved in creating the nektars within the body, which is perceived as both a temple and a laboratory, are painstaking to learn and involve working with what are known as the *Invisible Veins* and the *Interior Stars* or *Interior Roses*, which are similar but not identical to the meridian systems and chakras respectively. However, having made the commitment as I did, within just a few months I began to see why this path was talked about by my teachers as the *Via Vitae* or the Path of Life. These nektars were medicines, elixirs of regeneration, agents of deeper seeing and ecstasy, vehicles for exploring the hidden regions of the universe. Yea, these nektars were truly the food of the gods!

There are ten nektars, the last of which is named the Impossible Nektar and which is considered to be a supreme achievement to produce, for it is the simultaneous generation of menstrual blood and breast milk by a woman who is not with an infant still taking milk from her mother. The ichor milk is allowed to run into the ichor moon blood and in their mingling so the final nektar is created, a liquid of such potency that it has been claimed to have the power to resurrect the dead, or conversely slay a hostile adversary. It is both honey and sting. One who achieves the production of this nektar is bestowed the title of Black Widow, and it is here that the path of the 6 meets the path of the 8 and the hexagon becomes as one with the lemniscate.

As a teenager I had been a voracious reader of any and all manner of books concerned with religion and spirituality, and had even managed to hubristically plough through fourteen hundred pages of HP Blavatsky's extraordinary two-volume work *The Secret Doctrine*. In the final hours before emerging from my inky black cell I astonished myself with the apparently spontaneous arrival of a single sentence from this most weighty of tomes, words which burst forth from the depths of memory like a solitary firework bursting with fire in the night sky, momentarily illuminating its surroundings. The words could not have been more fitting, for Blavatsky had remarked that "darkness is the root of light, without which the latter could not exist." I leaned into and held onto these words as closely as I was able as I completed my final furlongs upon this charcoal path. And some months after my incubation was over I was drawn to track down that very quote only to discover it was longer and weightier than I had recalled. It continued thusly "Light is Matter and Darkness is pure Spirit. Darkness, in its radical, metaphysical basis, is subjective and absolute Light. While the latter, in all its searing effulgence and Glory, is merely a mass of shadows." In rediscovering these words I was now finally able to understand what I previously had thought I had comprehended.

The Living Power of Darkness

In the wake of my induction into darkness and my rebirth into physical light I eventually reengaged with my professional training as a young anthropologist, specifically now seeking to discover if the application of physical darkness formed a part of other native cultures and shamanic or folkloric traditions. Upon reviewing the anthropological and ethnographic literature, it became apparent that the phenomena of going into darkened places from just a few hours in some cases to a number of years in others was and indeed still is a cross-cultural phenomenon. Indeed, it is so universal that it seems baffling that the application of physical darkness within spiritual traditions today is so obscure. The following examples will, I hope, illustrate universality of the living power of living darkness:

Within Shinto, the indigenous spiritual tradition of Japan, the ascetic discipline of *komori* or seclusion is practiced, undertaken in the darkness of a cave, temple, shrine or even a room within the home that is specifically prepared and purified so it may bring the gift of power and illumination. The power-giving qualities of this type of dark seclusion are intriguing, for sacred power is seen as manifesting in darkness within a sealed vessel where it gestates and grows until it eventually bursts through its covering and emerges into the light of the world. This quality of an object containing supernatural power in the fruitful darkness it holds within it is known as *utsubo*, and the mythic gourds and fruits are its vessels. It is understood that before sacred power—as manifested in a being from another world—can burst its skin and appear in this world, it must first gestate in darkness. Likewise, the aspirant who wishes to acquire spiritual power must undergo gestation in the nearest approximation of an utsubo, be it a cave, shrine or darkened chamber. In the womblike stillness the aspirant fasts and recites prayers while darkness becomes the teacher.

On the other side of the world among the Dagara tribe of Burkina Faso in Africa, darkness is also perceived to be alive. Indeed, in common with other proto-historical tribes, the Dagara forbid any illumination of the darkness, for light is known to scare aware the spirits. Night is considered the "daytime" of these spirits and of the ancestors whose task it is to tell the Dagara what lies upon their life paths. Shedding light upon the darkness is thus akin to an insult to the spirits, a choice to ignore the opportunity they offer for illumination. When my dear colleague, the West African writer Malodoma Patrice Somé (who was born a Dagara but then was kidnapped and raised by Jesuit missionaries) returned to his tribe at age fifteen, he discovered that no one in the village wanted any form of light. Indeed, they were all expected to function in the dark. "I was given light because I had lost the ability to deal with darkness," he said. "And each time people saw the timid light of the oil lamp in my room, they would walk away from it as if it signaled the presence of someone playing with the elements of the cosmos. No one ever came to sit by me at night."

The Lakota Sioux of North America also regard the living landscape of darkness as the home of the spirits. Arguably their most powerful healing ceremony, still conducted to this day by Lakota shamans, is the *yuwipi*, which translates as "they wrap him up." The ceremony takes place in a room or a tent that has been totally darkened. The shaman is first wrapped tightly within a blanket and then bound with ropes all over his body, his hands tied together behind his back. He is then laid down upon a bed of sage brush and, during the ceremonial healing that follows, is freed from his bonds by his helping spirits, which often appear in the darkened room as moving or flashing blue lights. Having experienced this ceremony in the role of the bound shaman on two separate occasions, I can verify that the spirits can indeed arrive with sufficient power to unbind the brutally hogtied shaman, even having the courtesy to place the several meters of rope into a tidy pile!

In the Bön tradition of Tibet, a detailed system of working in darkness has also survived intact. Bön is Tibet's oldest spiritual tradition and as the indigenous source of Tibetan culture has played a unique role in shaping the country's identity. Within it, the faithful practice a forty-nine day darkness retreat during which the practitioner withdraws from external stimuli in order to have revealed to them a pathway leading to the totality of the self, being given a powerful means for bringing to light the deepest karmic obscurations of the mind as well as the opportunity to undertake preparations for undertaking a conscious death.

The Kogi Indians of the Sierra Nevada de Santa Marta in Colombia regard darkness as a vital tool for self-discovery and a vehicle of initiation for the elect into the priesthood of the tribe. For the Kogi, an individual is called to the priesthood through divination that is undertaken as soon as the child is born. If chosen, the infant is taken from his family and carried into the mountains where he is raised by the Kogi *Mamas* or priests where the child lives a nocturnal life, completely shut away from the sun, forbidden even to know the light of the moon. These chosen children remain in total darkness for up to nineteen years and in so doing acquire remarkable gifts of visioning and clairvoyance, capable of seeing not only into the future and the past but through all material illusions of the universe, learning to undertake journeys through the lands of the dead and into the hearts of the living.

In citing these few examples it should not be thought that engaging with the living darkness is an activity that happens within cultures other than our own. In Europe, as well as the 23-day initiatory experience in the hexagonal cell, there is ample proof of the importance that darkness played, from the retreats made by our Paleolithic ancestors of Western Europe within the caves of Lascaux, Chauvet and Altamira, to the rituals of Mithraism which took place within the windowless caverns or Mithraea, to the darkened chambers of temple sleep that occurred within the temple of Asclepius at Epidaurus and elsewhere.

What may be of particular interest to readers is that the tradition of our European ancestors entering into darkness carried on into the modern era in Northern Europe within not just the Path of Pollen, but elsewhere as well. Best documented is the tradition of the Irish poets engaging with darkness to receive inspiration. And it is well worth noting that the Gaelic poet—the *file*—was viewed as a deeply shamanic figure bestowed with many of the same skills and responsibilities, which could include word doctoring, divination, blessing and cursing. Much as the professions of history, law and medicine were confined to certain families, so the *file* belonged to a hereditary caste. The Gaelic poet was both born and made, with the six to seven-year training involving the practice of *lighe a leapthaibh both* or "lying in the beds of booths." According to an account from 1722, the typical poet lay in an unlit hut working out his verses "upon his own bed in the dark."

Like the shaman, the Gaelic poet was seen as a mystic who was able to see the light of inspiration in the darkness and have darkness as a muse from whence the inspiration arose.

Over the last thirty-three years I have regularly undertaken darkness retreats, the longest of which has been the aforementioned 23 days. For the last fifteen years I have been taking small groups with me to explore this benighted, tenebrous path. From what Carl Jung, a shaman in all but name, secretly wrote within *The Red Book* which was not published until 2009, it would seem that he, too, spent time exploring the value of the living darkness. His words echo what many modern explorers into this meta-womb have discovered:

"The darkness is your mother; she behooves reverence, since the mother is dangerous. She has power over you, since she gave birth to you. Honor the darkness as the light, and you will illumine your darkness. If you comprehend the darkness, it seizes you. It comes over you like the night with black shadows and countless shimmering stars. Silence and peace come over you if you begin to comprehend the darkness. Only he who does not comprehend the darkness fears the night."

The shaman, one who "sees in the dark," might postulate that there is ultimately no such thing as darkness, but merely the inability to truly see. Darkness itself is healing and nurturing and paradoxically allows us perhaps the greatest opportunity to become a witness to our own radiance, our own inner light and the greater luminosity of our personal souls.

The Gift

Having created an endarkened space, whether via pilgrimage to a cave, the blacking out of a room in your home or simply awaiting the arrival of midnight, the journey to what has been referred to by the ancients as the *midnight sun* is commenced by a formula of murmured prayer-chant in which certain words are rhythmically repeated again and again, whilst other words are arrived at spontaneously. The continuous repetition is important, and those words are: *I am as a vessel of darkness*....which is then followed by spontaneous examples of what flows through you as that vessel. Herewith a small number of examples:

I am as a vessel of darkness and night skies flow through me.

I am as a vessel of darkness and the stars they flow through me.

I am as a vessel of darkness and forests flow through me.

I am as a vessel of darkness and my ancestors flow through me.

I am as a vessel of darkness and darkness flows through me.

Periods of activity (the chanting) should be followed by periods of active silence in which the sub-vocal self-command of *"surrender"* is given. That is, in those silent moments you seek to engage in the paradox of *actively* surrendering into the compassionate arms of darkness herself. If a complete and utter surrender is accomplished, the greatest of gifts may be proffered: the veil is removed from the concealed light of true gnosis, which itself can bring about a rebirth of the self as one who is now truly the new pearl of great price.

Journey well pilgrim! Let the words of Robertus de Fluctibus see you on your way: "Darkness adopted illumination to make itself visible."

Bibliography:

Blavatsky, Helena Petrovna. The Secret Doctrine, Theosophical Publishing House, Madras, 1888

Buxton, Simon. *Darkness Visible*, Destiny Books, Vermont, 2005

The Shamanic Way of the Bee, Destiny Books, Vermont, 2003

Cloutier, David. *Spirit Spirit: Shaman Songs Incantations,* Copper Beech Press, 1973

Eliade, Mircea. *The Sacred and The Profane*, Harcourt Brace & Co, New York, 1959

Harner, Michael. *Cave and Cosmos*, North Atlantic Books, 2013.

Hultkrantz, Åke. *Spirit Lodge, a North American Séance*. Studies in Shamanism: 32-68, Almquist & Wiksell, Stockholm, 1967

Jung, Carl G. *The Red Book (Liber Novus),* W.W. Norton, New York, 2009.

Osborn Bergin. *Irish Bardic Poetry*, The Dublin Institute for Advanced Studies, Dublin, 1970

Shirokogoroff, S.M. *Social Organization of the Northern Tungus,* Garland Publishers, 1929

Somé, Malodoma Patrice. *Of Water and Spirit: Ritual, Magic and Initiation in the Life of an African Shaman.* New York: Tarcher/Putnam, 1994

CHAPTER 4

Gogo Ekhaya Esima was born in the United States and is an initiated Sangoma Traditional Healer in the Shangaan and Zulu lineages of Southern Africa. She is a certified Mental Health Recovery Specialist, a trauma survivor, and a spiritual teacher. Her own experience with mental health crisis and her at times frightening at times profoundly beautiful journey through it eventually led her deeply into traditional African spirituality.

A strong advocate for challenging standardized mental health concepts in America, her work has allowed her to represent the underserved in the US Mental Health System by speaking at universities, conferences, and summits across the country. She leads ceremonies around the world and has written for the soon to be published academic book *Women & Psychosis.* Gogo Ekhaya openly shares her shamanic journey of healing and recovery in the feature-length, award-winning documentary, *Crazywise.*

In her work, she addresses the importance of ancestral healing, a supportive community, and other integral aspects of traditional African life and values that are specific to the healing process of our collective consciousness and liberation. Gogo Ekhaya currently works in service as a full-time traditional healer in Southern California.

She can be reached at sangomahealing.com

The Sangoma Way

From my earliest memories, I've always felt connected to nature and felt a deep sense of spirituality throughout my life. At about seven-years old, in the middle of the night, I opened my eyes and saw a human-like figure with wings and a bright glow emanating from it standing in front of my bedroom door. I quickly shut my eyes and opened them several times, rubbing them to confirm what I was seeing.

My childhood was full of dreams that would come to pass in my waking life. I began to notice that the things that I sensed about people were usually true. For instance, I dreamt of a prominent TV personality who was loved internationally. But I saw his dark side in my dreams as an abuser of women. This was, of course, confirmed later when news broke about all the women he'd harmed. I also sensed negative energies about people near to my family. One of them was later imprisoned for robbing a bank. In the late hours of the night, I would experience my bed shaking and spinning in what felt like a circular vortex. In an attempt to feel connected to this world, I would bounce my legs up and down on the bed to help me feel safe and decrease my anxiety. This experience happened so frequently it became the norm. Much later in life, I came to see the connection between these experiences and shamanic dreaming as well as astral traveling.

My mom left my dad when I was little, but I saw him at least every week. He was this big, 6'1" creative giant—a poet, a chef, a teacher, and an amazing artist. I was always inspired by his vast knowledge and it seemed like he knew a little about everything. He also held very high expectations of me with my education, and when I didn't live up to them he was verbally aggressive which caused me to be fearful and filled with anxiety. And when he drank on the nights of my sleepovers, the moral boundaries of our relationship blurred. I liked this man during the day. But at night the alcohol took precedence. I don't remember a time when the touching and molestation weren't present.

The Impact of Western Medicine and Finding My Purpose

As I grew older, these wounding experiences produced suppressed emotions and toxic belief patterns which eventually lead to what Western medicine would diagnose as psychosis. I heard voices in my head telling me lies, telling me to harm myself by cutting my arms to help relieve my pain. When I got married and started a family, it became extremely hard for me to deal with the pain that I was carrying inside. Being intimate with my husband, I would see my father's face and push him off of me in anger. During two of my pregnancies I became severely depressed and suicidal. I was afraid to breastfeed because of my damaged perspective on intimacy. I became extremely depressed and my relationship with my children became progressively unstable. Eventually I divorced.

The thought of ending my life never went away. When a challenge or hardship arose it was the place that I went to, the solution to the chaos around and within me. I tried therapy a few times and gave up because I never felt a connection or sensed that my experiences were truly understood. In my early twenties I started taking psychiatric drugs outside of inpatient treatment and felt foggy and emotionally disconnected to everything around me, including my children. Later I tried self-medicating and created other addictive patterns to self soothe. The visions came back, but now the voices in my head became loud enough to manipulate me to self-harm. I ended up in a vicious cycle of being locked in psych units after suicidal attempts and was even homeless at one point.

Fortunately, one particular hospital offered art therapy, tai chi, and also had a visiting monk who led meditation groups. Finally, I was able to connect to something familiar within myself—a touch of spirit memory within the fog of all the heavily sedating psychotropic drugs and sleeping pills.

One day, while sitting in meditation, I had a pleasant vision of a scarab beetle and a wolf. In art therapy I painted what I had witnessed and later researched what these animals might mean from a Native American animal totem/spirit perspective. As it turned out, beetles symbolize the ability to survive, transform and rebirth. The wolf's message is balance, harmony, inner knowing and new beginnings. Both these messages resonated with my spirit and in them I found inspiration. Wolf and beetle became my guides into a rite of passage. I could almost taste the transformation to come.

Sangoma Initiation

Rite of passage in traditional African culture is a ceremonial process that everyone in the tribe goes through. Here, in the West, we miss this opportunity to be held in sacred space during times of transition.

Which means some of us get dragged, pushed, and thrown into states of spiritual emergence, completely unaware of their significance to our life's purpose. My ultra-sensitivities were a major part of a gift that wanted to emerge. In retrospect, I was definitely being guided by spirit to awaken the whole time. But having no spiritual guidance, I had no way of recognizing what was happening to me.

After my last therapeutic programs, I was introduced to the concept of "Peers" working in mental health—individuals with lived experiences acting as counselors, advocates, and supporters to those suffering with mental health challenges. I became a Peer Specialist myself, and began my journey into alternative healing modalities. I researched shamanism, indigenous cultures, and was deeply moved in my spirit to consult with a Sangoma Traditional Healer. During the consultation I learned that I had ancestors with me that needed help. Some of them had experienced historical traumas and these deeply rooted memories were being passed from generation to generation without being recognized and healed. I was also informed that there were powerful ancestral guardians in my blood lineage who were calling me to carry on their healing traditions and spiritual rituals in this lifetime.

The first time that I went to the Sangoma's ndumba (house of the ancestors) was for a healing session. I walked in and saw initiates kneeling on the floor, eyes focused towards the ground. They all wore similar clothing. They smudged me with smoke and offered me water. The Sangoma came into the room, full of grace and warm smiles. She welcomed me and asked if I'd sit in the living room to wait while they prepared a few things.

As I sat there, I could feel a crowd of spirits around me. Drumming and strange sounds were coming from the other room. One of the initiates lead me into the sacred shrine. A veil of smoke danced around the darkly-lit room from the burning of herbs. I was told to kneel and present my offerings to the ancestors. Then the drumming began and the room filled with beautiful Zulu songs that penetrated my heart with a deep resonance.

I began to feel really heavy, as if some unseen body were sitting on top of me. Soon my face was on the floor, my legs stretched out. I no longer had control over my body. A movement of fiery energy began to make its way up from the depths of my belly up my throat. My mouth opened wide to spew an unknown archaic ritual language. The drum became louder, the sounds of the sacred rattle sweeping against my eardrums. I could not think, only surrender.

The night was long. When I came out of trance, the Sangoma had deciphered the message from the Ancestors. (Sangomas are expert seers and spirit listeners.) I was being called to the Sangoma traditional path. From that point on I would be leaving the life of suffering I had painfully clung to for the past 15 years. Trusting the guidance of my ancestral tribe and their voices, I decided to say "yes" to this calling, and the Sangoma, Yeye Gogo Nana Iyalode, became my teacher or Baba (parent).

Initiates are to sacrifice simple pleasures of the mind and body in order to connect to the spirits of the ancestors, medicines and ancient secrets. This includes sleep deprivation, a special diet, plant medicine intake, seclusion, no physical or sexual contact and much more. These sacrifices are imposed to induce a deep experience of humility and a shedding of the old identify of self. Initiates also have an intense and strict schedule of prayer times, trance dance, and cleansing. Opening up the communication line to the divine guardians includes spiritual cleansing through bathing with medicine, inhaling smoke from herbs, and drinking medicine that allows one to purge negative energies under the watchful eye of the teacher with the guidance of our spirit and plant allies. Your character, integrity and dedication are challenged continuously in order for you to grow and become a carrier of this ancient wisdom. Not surprisingly, in South Africa, many people resist the calling to initiate as a Sangoma because it's such a difficult process. If they resist, the spiritual gifts tend to haunt them throughout their lives, causing many disruptions such as bad luck, prolonged illnesses, and feelings of disconnection.

With Sangoma initiation (ukuthwasa), the calling chooses you, one cannot simply choose it. Governed by the ancestral spirits that called you, it is they who decide when the initiate is ready to become a Sangoma. The calling also comes through a bloodline or foreign ancestor who once lived as a medicine healer who wishes to pass down their shamanic wisdom to you. I was possessed with the energy of a man I was shown in dreams and visions, who lived long ago in Southern Africa. My iDlozi spirit was the guardian passing the shamanic wisdom to me through my blood lineage.

Normally a thwasa (an initiate) leaves their home for many months or years to go live with their teacher. That way they don't have to deal with outside distractions, like work and family life, while integrating with their iDlozi spirit. This is important because the portals to the spirit world are open and you are always going in and out of this physical realm to the next. This should happen in a safe container until you gain the ability to ground and control your spiritual travels.

Because of my commitments, I did not have the opportunity to live with my Baba full-time. During the intense process of integrating with my ancestral guardian spirits, while out in the world, I'm sure I sometimes looked like what some would perceive as a "crazy person." Involuntary movements, spontaneous trance states, and foreign sounds (like burping and grunting for instance!) were some of the exterior symptoms as the strong, fiery spirit of my ancestor merged within me. It also had to assist me in getting rid of the lower-level spirits or energies that were with me, drawn by my past pain and dissociation from trauma and all the medications—not an easy or pleasant process to watch.

Some of the mastery techniques included the daily ritual of communicating with the guardian Ancestors, and through that communication opening portals for the Ancestors to emerge through the body. This particular ritual changed my perspective of people out in public seemingly in full conversation to someone or something unseen. The difference is, those people haven't had the opportunity to refine their communication in a sacred way.

Unlike what a lot of people think, initiation is not glamorous. It is a very serious and highly challenging process. When I underwent ukuthwasa, I was in a trance state for several months on a consistent basis. Since the initiation process is meant to awaken the sleeping ones within, a thwasa is always moving and active in order to keep the energy of their guiding ancestral spirits awake. It was very difficult to go to work and do daily activities and be grounded! Luckily, I was supported by my fellow peer counselors during this transformation and had access to vacation time when needed.

But even when I became terribly sleep deprived, I rarely had thoughts of quitting. Initiation felt like a matter of life or death. I was acutely aware how important humility was to both my Baba and my guardian spirits—a value that becomes the essence of the Sangoma's lifestyle and work.

Towards the end of training there is a particular ritual where an unknown object is hidden from you. The initiate has to use their gift of hearing voices, seeing or sensing to correctly identify the object missing and it's exact location. The twaza does not complete initiation until this process is tested thoroughly and successfully. The repetition of this work allowed me to trust and build a great connection with the voices of my guardian ancestors. The trust in my gift and in myself became stronger as I continued to take part in the rituals and medicines.

This was the turning point for me. I was healing, and all that was sick in my mind was now becoming liberated into an amazing yet humbling gift.

Sangoma Medicine

One day Baba took us to the river to cleanse. Before I even stepped foot in the water I could feel the spirits of nature surrounding me. I was swept into a trance state and was pulled towards a beautiful tree on the other side of the river bank that was calling me. The water was just low enough that day to show where the tree's roots were exposed. My Ancestor's voice came through me and started speaking an ancient language to the tree. The tree spirit listened, and I reached my hands up to touch its roots. My body shook as if lighting had struck. I intuitively knew that the tree spirit and the sacred waters were collectively working to de-possess me from lower level spirits and attachments that I had accumulated from my sexual abuse in childhood and from being ultra-sensitive to energies throughout my life without the proper spiritual protection or guidance. All that energy was being washed away in the river while the spirit of the tree shocked me into strength, vitality, and the ancient remembrance of ancestral power.

In African spirituality, we recognize that the elements of the Earth have a spirit and vibration that reside within it. We also understand that the Ancestors reside in the forces of nature and use the elements to communicate with us or act as allies. I was guided to take a small piece of the tree's roots to use as medicine. This experience opened me up to the mystical world of plant medicines and the awesome and sophisticated intelligence of nature. Trees and plants communicate with us when we are open to listening. They tell us stories. And when we humbly give gratitude they reveal secrets of their medicinal gifts and powers.

As in all indigenous healing traditions, the Sangoma learns how to communicate with these beings. We learn what offerings to make to honor these majestic spirits of the land. We call sacred healing plants, roots, and herbs "umuthi." Muthi can be used to heal, to protect, and to strengthen the spirit. They are applied through steaming techniques, lineaments, smoke inhaled, ingested, bathed in, snuffed, or applied directly into the bloodstream through tiny incisions made in the skin. We use muthi to obtain particular outcomes for a patient, such as cleansing particular ancestral spirits, success in legal matters, healing the heart or trauma, or opening one up to the dream world.

There are specific umuthi that only initiates use to help them during their process and connection to the Ancestors. One very important muthi used by the Sangoma is *The Telepathic Connection*/Imphepho (Helichrysum odoratissimum). Imphepho is a sacred herb burned in ceremonial spaces and inhaled by the Sangoma to communicate with the Ancestral guardians for divination. It is also used like salvia officinalis (sage) to clear energy.

When a patient comes to consult with a Sangoma, a specific form of divination is used as a spiritual and physical diagnostic tool. Some Sangomas use bone divination, others use water, or bang special muthi sticks to divine and connect to their ancestral guardians. Once the guardians have been invoked, the Sangoma can read the patient and tell them what is happening with the mind, body, and spirit. A spiritual prescription is most likely given to the patient in order to resolve any issues.

This is where umuthi can come in. Based on the results from the reading, we create a healing story to counteract the illness or troubles by combining medicines and through ritual allow the patient to be healed and overcome problems. Some umuthi are titled by specific phrases based on its medicinal and spiritual powers. For example *Dispeller of Parasitic*

Spirits / Aloe Ferox, is a powerful indigenous muthi used for removing negative spirit attachments as well as detoxifying the body. It is also used in snuff mixtures with other muthi to clear overactive thoughts and to still the mind.

Calm the Heart & Mind / Kanna, is used by chewing on the bitter bark to help relieve panic, anxiety, and help elevate mood. Sangomas also use Kanna as a divining instrument. *Awaken to Life* is used for psychosomatic issues, for depression, emotional pain, and heartbreak to bring a person "back to life" from sorrow and suffering. *Wipe It Clean* is used as an aura cleanser. The patient will bathe with this medicine, inducing an intense itching sensation to remove unwanted energetic debris picked up by others. *Illuminate from Afar* is used to help bring light energy closer to you and attract beautiful vibrations. For example, you could use it before a speaking engagement or a job interview.

There are thousands of umuthi used in the Sangoma traditions of southern Africa that have been used for millennia to keep communities healthy and spiritually balanced. Sacred dream medicine is also used for initiates into the Sangoma tradition. Dreams are one of the most important ways to obtain enlightenment and get to the completion of the process to become a Sangoma. Dreams are shared between teacher and student and examined thoroughly. Only certain dreams will let the teacher know what the student needs, what rituals are done next for the process and when they are ready for a completion ceremony.

Presently, over 60 percent of the South African population seek Sangomas for healing of physical, mental, emotional, and spiritual issues. Sangomas are recognized by the government as bona fide traditional doctors. There are as many as 200,000 indigenous traditional healers in South Africa as compared to 25,000 Western-trained doctors.

Traditional Medicine in a Western World

In my work it is important for me to maintain the traditional ways that the ancestors before me lived. And yet I have found that it is also important to change with the times and consult the spirits regularly as to how to keep the essence of our traditions intact while adjusting to environmental needs to preserve the overuse of vulnerable plant medicines and respect the impermanence of nature.

On the flip side, there needs to be an awakening within the Western medical community as to the realities of energy, unseen influences, and the vital importance of acknowledging spiritual crisis and spiritual realities. About a year after becoming a Sangoma Traditional Healer, I was working in an organization that supports people diagnosed with Severe Mental Illness (SMI). When I picked up one of my peer clients to take her to her psychiatric appointment, she was in what I would call a trance state, speaking in an unfamiliar language. While filling out her paperwork, she reached out her hand and touched me.

Instantly, I felt dizzy and uneasy in my body. I tried my best to be present with her, but it was impossible. I asked a coworker to take over and went to get some water. But when I stood up my knees were weak and there was intense pressure on my back such that I walked bent over like an elderly person. I made it to the restroom, splashed water on my face, then went outside to try and ground myself. Nothing worked. I was headed to the other realms. When I returned to my desk my body began to shake uncontrollably like I was having a seizure. I could not speak or control any aspect of my physical body, including my voice and eyes.

I knew what had happened. When the woman touched me, an energy transference occurred. I needed to go home and deal with it immediately through ceremony. But my co-workers called the paramedics. Because my vital signs were fine, the paramedics didn't believe I really couldn't speak or control my body. As a result, I ended up at the hospital being seen by a doctor on the psych ward threatening to drug me with Ativan to "calm me down."

Mind you, I hadn't been on prescription drugs for almost three years. The thought of being injected made old experiences in the psych wards resurface. Finally, I mustered up the energy to say, "No, I work as a mental health counselor. I refuse treatment. I know my rights. You cannot force treatment on me. I want to go home."

Visibly annoyed, the doctor said, "I'm giving you an injection." An argument ensued. Finally he stalked off in disgust and I was wheeled back into the emergency holding room. More problems occurred when the nurses told me I had to take off my sacred beads. Thankfully, an African doctor from Nigeria came in. Our interaction was the complete opposite to the intake doctor. He agreed to speak to my Baba and, after his assessment and a few hours in the ER, he released me to go home where I took care of the situation.

This experience was a shock and an enormous reminder of how important it is to educate people—especially medical professionals—about spiritual emergency. It also forced me into realizing I was done with the Western model of "healing." I had to work from a place of spiritual understanding and the shamanic wisdom I had gained through my own transformation. Immediately I quit my job and started my work as a full-time Sangoma and headed to the mountains of California. Today I am living out my purpose and it is a humbling experience to see my journey reflected in those who come for spiritual and ancestral healing. There is a deep level of compassion and joy that I feel, witnessing people coming out of their storm and awakening to their wellbeing and the gifts of life.

By breaking free of the confines of the medical-model, I am now able to utilize my own experiences and Peer Recovery skill to assist others from around the world with mental imbalances, combining these Western techniques with ancient healing modalities. To me this is true whole-person care. It is my prayer that, not too far in the future, Western medicine will begin to acknowledge the importance of addressing patients' spiritual needs in order to bring about purpose in their lives as well as mental, emotional and physical recovery.

The Gift

In this modern world it is vital for us to stay connected to nature. A water cleansing ritual is a powerful tool for spiritual maintenance and overall well-being. Water is the vibrational essence of our bodies and we bathe, consume, and release it daily.

Here is a simple ritual to stay connected to nature and heighten your relationship with this plentiful element.

Water ritual: While in the shower, say a prayer of gratitude to the divine water element before turning the water on. While the water is running, ask the divine element of water to bring you clarity and purification for your day. Repeat the words, *I release, I cleanse, I heal* and be present with the sensation of the water on your body the entire time. Give thanks at the end of your cleansing of mind, body, and of spirit. You may also do this before drinking a glass of water in the morning or during a meditation while honoring the water element already within you for healing.

CHAPTER 5

Wayne D. Carter was born in Anchorage Alaska. At an early age he started seeing spirits and being aware of interdimensional energies. "As a kid I wanted world peace and also a Hot Wheels," he says. "I wanted the world to be different, to be kind and respectful. So, I've made a career of treating people as individual human beings rather than labels. If I catch myself being a normal, poorly socially-conditioned male, I seek support and mentorship to change my behavior."

At age 32 he embraced his Seminole roots and began working with an Inuit Huron Medicine Man of Ojibway/Huron ancestry, learning Native American healing ways. After working with him for 16 years, he was introduced to the Sun Dance and the Blackfoot tribal ways in Alberta, Canada. He has Sun Danced for 17 years and counts among the great blessings of his life the right to use healing plants, the right to lead ceremonies, the right to use the pipe, the right to fast, the right to sweat, and the right to pour at sweat lodges. To keep a roof over his head, gasoline in his truck and dogfood in the dog bowl, he works as a carpenter.

For more information please contact:
www.onepassionlove.com

Rights of Passage: Sun Dancing and Salvation

The first time I remember seeing spirits was the night after a few other kids and I decided to dig a hole to China in the backyard of my house in Eugene, Oregon. We didn't get to China, but after going down about three feet, we did discover arrowheads, pottery, and other Native American artifacts. Of course, we grabbed at the treasure, trading stuff back and forth until everybody had what they wanted. Then my friends went home, leaving me standing silent and dazed beside the pile of freshly-turned earth, a knapped piece of flint in hand, oddly transformed by my proximity to the real natives of the land I called home. I was five.

That night, while trying to sleep, I saw a shadow moving across my bedroom wall. I looked more closely and saw that it was actually many shadows in a row, like a group of people walking down a path. Terrified, I yelled at the top of my lungs until my parents ran into the room and turned on the light. Of course, like pretty much all parents, they proceeded to hug and comfort me, telling me it was "just a nightmare." As soon as they left the room, I saw the bodies moving again and shrieked. This happened several times with my parents getting more and more frustrated with each episode. Finally, I stopped crying out and just watched the spirits on the wall, as terrified of my parents' anger as I was of the shadows.

Another unforgettable experience occurred when I was nine-years old. We'd moved down to Fullerton, California into an old stucco house. To get to my bedroom, you took a left down a long hallway that ran the length of the house. On the right side of the hallway was a closet. When we moved in, I found a knife, a Bible, and a skeleton key in that closet. Sounds like setup for a movie plot. But I swear I'm not making this up.

One night, shortly after moving in, I heard a voice coming from the end of the hall near the closet. I could see the closet door from my bedroom, and watched in terror as a spirit in the form of a skeleton opened the door and stood there, looking directly at me. Then he turned and disappeared back into the closet, closing the door behind him. I lay there waiting for something else to happen, but nothing did.

After several weeks of this scene repeating itself every night, I started to relax. (Amazing what you can get used to as a kid.) Then one night the unthinkable happened. Instead of going back into the closet, the skeleton shut the closet door and walked down the hall into my bedroom, straight towards me, taking a right at the foot of the bed and standing at the left side of the footboard. I started screaming in terror. My mother was the first to arrive.

"What is it?"

I pointed my shaking finger at the skeleton spirit beside my bed and whispered, "That!"

She took one look and fainted, hitting the floor with a loud thud. I screamed even harder then, because whatever it was did not leave. My father dashed in and lifted my mother onto the bed. The spirit left sometime during all this commotion and I never saw it again in that house.

Up until a few years ago, my mom denied seeing anything. Finally she fessed up over a Mother's Day dinner in Puyallup. "Remember when you pointed to that thing in your bedroom that night as a kid?"

"You mean in California?"

"Yes." After a very long pause, she admitted seeing something that night. She was still unable to make sense of it, or articulate what she saw. Nevertheless, I felt validated that she would bring it up after all those decades had passed. But it made me sad that our conversation hadn't happened four decades earlier when it could have done a young boy good.

I still see spirits on a regular basis, and rely on insights from the other world in my practice as a shaman, healer and seminar leader. But sometimes I wonder how much more developed my intuition might be today if my parents had had an awareness and understanding of paranormal abilities. Those lonely, fearful years of childhood could have been a lot happier and less confusing if my parents had *just once* considered that I was telling the truth about what I saw, heard and felt. As it was, they were rational adults who found my paranormal gifts weird and creepy, or worse, simply a crazed bid for attention.

Most parents teach their children at a very young age to block psychic images—which is, of course, why 30 years later adults have such a hard time opening their minds to the possibility of non-physical realms. This sends a not-so-veiled message that children should mistrust what they actually experience and rely on adult reality instead. At the same time, it robs children of a sense of self-trust they will desperately need to find balance, not only in a world of increasing chaos, but in their own heads, learning to discern and sort Earthly versus inter-dimensional information as it comes at them.

I had to learn not to discount what I was experiencing, even though there was all that adult authority weighing in, constantly saying. "It's just your imagination." Which leaves you alone in the dark with things going bump in the night, scared out of your wits, wondering about your sanity.

I tried to learn how to turn my psychic receptivity on and off. But apparently I just dammed it up. By the time I was in my thirties the psychic backlog was overflowing and I started to have a lot more stuff happen. I saw spirits—like a guy in a top hat and tails walking down the street—in broad daylight. Sometimes the world would shapeshift. I would be driving east toward the mountains and I would stop because Mount Rainier (a massive 14,411-foot volcano in Washington State) was suddenly not in the right place. Or the world around me would suddenly shrink, looking minuscule, like I was looking down at a Monopoly board.

In the early 1990s these visions were happening so frequently, making life so difficult, that I basically knocked on the front door of the Western Washington State Mental Hospital in Steilacoom and tried to commit myself. But the psychiatrist doing the interview said based on my history and what I was experiencing that I wasn't a candidate. When I told him my grandfather was full-blood Seminole on my father's side he gently advised that I see somebody traditional who could help me through this.

Thus, Robert, an Inuit Huron Medicine Man of Ojibway/Huron ancestry, came into my life. At first I was very frightened to talk about the stuff that was going on. But quickly I discovered he knew exactly what I was talking about. He'd even finish the stories I was telling him as if he'd been there, which freaked me out as much as anything else I'd experienced.

"You have a gift," he said. "You are an intuitive visionary and capable of doing healing work. But you haven't had the support and training you should have had starting back in childhood. You aren't integrated and you haven't yet learned to be humble."

Robert worked with me for 16 years, teaching me the ways of the pipe, the ways of healing, gathering the plants and stones to use in healing ceremonies. He helped me learn how to talk with the spirits about what a person needs to heal. He taught me how to listen to my own song. He was also instrumental in getting me to my first Sun Dance.

A Needed Humbling

I was invited to the first Sun Dance up in Alberta, Canada somewhere on a farm in the middle of nowhere. I drove on a bunch of back gravel roads straight to the farm drive without any directions whatsoever. Somebody met me at the gates, saying, "Oh, you're Wayne? We've been waiting for you. Come on in."

I am honor-bound by the traditions I've been accepted into not to talk about the Sun Dance itself, its exact location or name any names of the people involved. But I can talk about the things that are public, my own experiences, and the lessons I've learned in the 17 years I've been Sun Dancing.

The first year I was there they allowed the public

to do "flesh offerings," a kind of mini-Sun Dance that lasts five minutes instead of four days, where they stick a needle in your skin and pull out a little piece and then cut it off with a scalpel. Participating in the flesh offering that day was an unexpected honor!

Over the years, the only time I've ever really experienced pain in the dance was when I was offering up somebody else's prayers, "honoring the rope" of a man who didn't complete his dance. It's hurts because you're basically taking on their karma—their energy—the things they've gone into the dance to pray for. But it's a sacrifice the teachers (those dancers who have completed at least four dances) are more than willing to make.

I cried watching that first Sun Dance in the summer of 2001. I didn't watch the men. I just watched the tree and the ropes flying through the air because of the tension and the snapping sounds. I knew I was home. I knew that sound. During that dance proceedings I was introduced to the Sun Dance leader and later to his wife. I didn't realize it at the time, but I'd just met my next teachers who would be my spiritual mentors for the next 17 years. That fall I went back to ask permission to fast, offering him gifts. He invited me into the preparation fast and it was the toughest thing I've ever done—four days with no food, no water, and five full hot sweats. Afterwards I went back to him with gifts and asked permission to dance and my request was granted.

The next summer, in 2002, I approached the Sun Dance grounds with great anticipation and confidence. I'd done all of this training with Robert. I'd been initiated into running trainings in Native

American traditions. I'd been given the rights to make plant medicines to help people and was doing my healing work. I was in great physical shape and going to sweat lodges. Somebody had even gifted me an eagle feather fan. Arriving many days before the dance, I helped with the preparations, cutting the trees for the arbor ... everything was perfect. And then the spirits just basically handed me my ass.

I don't even remember getting up to the point where they dragged me out of the arbor because I blacked out. I left my body and was so far out of the world they had no idea where I was. After I came back to my body it took more than a day to get my heartrate under 70-80 beats a minute! The following year I made it through most of the dance. But again, another man had to honor my rope and take on my prayers and finish my dance for me. The fourth year I recommitted and it was like being in bliss the entire dance.

My nephew was in prison on a felony charge— he'd been in and out of jail since he was a kid— so during that dance I was praying for him. After the dance everybody had left and I went out into the arbor and went down on my knees. I was just looking at the tree and as I started to speak my prayers it was like I could hear my voice echoing across the hills and mountains. I stood up and looked around and the arbor was full of spirits. Not people in regalia, but people in jeans and T-shirts. Some I met later on and some I never met. It was like they were witnessing my prayer. Then I went off into the wilderness for a month or so to integrate my experience.

Not long afterwards the judge let my nephew

out of his 16-year sentence after a year and a half. He went to college and got married. Now he's running his own business in California, has his own apartment, and mentors street people.

There's a part of the Sun Dance where you can offer to take on someone's prayers or offer yourself as sacrifice for someone's healing. During one dance I remember this old Native woman who could barely make it to the arbor. People had to help her out of the truck. During the dance I offered to do what is termed "pulling skulls" for her, and she went from sitting to standing up the first round. The next guy pulled skulls for her and she went from wobbly to moving back and forth. Then I pulled skulls for her again and when I broke, thunder and lightning happened in the sky. The timing was rather interesting! She started dancing, then walked back out of the arbor to her truck and climbed in by herself.

In 2014, the summer after my head injury (I'd been in an auto accident) I danced and saw these two eagles fly down from the tree. They grabbed me by the shoulders and took me up into the Sun Dance tree, pulling the burden of all my drama out of my life. For three years I sat with that vision and in 2017 I honored that vision by being pierced and pulled up into the trees.

Every dance has been huge. And it is not always the dance that's been huge. It's also all the tradition and ceremonies. It's the spirit in which these traditions are followed, the spirit in which the ceremonies are offered, and the lessons that are learned. For years I would come to the Sun Dance fields weeks early and stay late, trying to do everything in a genuine desire to help. But I was also doing it to be accepted. Oh, how I wanted to be seen as worthy! It took years for the Sun Dance leaders, my teachers, to gradually show me that I had to discover my own worth. That it wasn't all about who could chop the most wood for the sweat lodges, or who could pour the sweats, or who could pull skulls.

All of my personal stories came up, like learning to deal with men. My dad was violent and abusive, physically, sexually, and emotionally. The dance helped me learn how to deal with guys. To understand how they can bark at each other and still love each other and get along. I learned I didn't have to hide my gifts in order to not push people's buttons. The dances worked me through all those things. I also learned to receive—something men aren't generally too good at. Amongst the great blessings of my life have been receiving the right to lead ceremonies, the right to fast, the right to sweat, the right to use the pipe, the right to dance, the right to pour at a sweat lodge.

I learned patience. My first Sun Dance, my teacher took me up into the mountains a couple weeks before the dance. One afternoon he pointed to a tree, a Balsam Fir, and said, "That would be a good smudge for you." I went back up that road into the mountains for five years and couldn't find that tree. The sixth year I found it and cut a small piece and the elders said, "Ah, you found it." At that point I was also given my tribal name, Pine Forest Boy. At first, I had a hard time with the boy part. I'm a man, after all. But in Blackfoot culture being a boy isn't a bad thing. It just means you're young, that you're learning. And there were definitely things I needed to learn before that tree would reveal itself. Plants show up when you need them. So does everything else in life.

It's definitely not a Western approach to learning.

Right of Passage

Rights of passage for males have mostly been lost or emasculated in modern Western culture. But initiations are absolutely essential for males because they need much tempering before they can approach being powerful like women. This isn't something you'll hear spoken about very often nowadays. It's something I learned from the old, old elders. Frankly, I wish I could get into this more deeply without creating a brouhaha. But I can't. So, let me just say that basically the Sun Dance and most other Native ceremonies for men are about humbling the men and getting them into a softer more intuitive, receptive space.

The way I've been trained, traditionally, women have carried the medicine in the ceremonies. Women have power that men don't have. They have a knowing. They're close to nature. If you send a woman out to get roots, she'll pick one here and pick one a half block down the road and then another one even further on. If you send a guy out to get roots, he takes a shovel and digs a hole five-feet wide. Guys have to learn how to be sensitive and aware like women.

As a man who has spent more than 30 years working in a healing capacity both with humans and animals, I recognize that the initiation into Western male adulthood has been reduced to a loud fight between dad and son, at which point, dad pats his son on the back and treats him as a man. This style of initiation is also used in the prison system. As an offender, others will challenge you initially to see if you will stand up for yourself.

(Standing up does not mean winning the fight, but rather being willing to take a stand for your own wellness, safety, health, etc.) If you do, you're in. If you don't, you're chopped liver.

My prayer today is for a healthy Right of Passage for young men to be introduced into the modern Western world, a rite along the lines of the following initiation used by the Blackfoot tribe in Southern Alberta.

It all starts with the mom. The first thing she does is watch how the elders in the community live their lives. Do their values and spiritual practices follow tradition? Are they involved with the community and ceremonies? Do they drink or do drugs or beat their wife? Do they hunt and take care of their home?

After she chooses a male elder she thinks fit for her son, she arranges a meeting with him to offer gifts and ask if he will mentor her boy. The elder will often think on this for a while and let her know when he feels the time is right for her son. The reason the father cannot do this is because of family power struggles and possible emotional wounds. Plus, this process allows a mother to share in the transition of her son to manhood, giving her the formal opportunity to grieve the loss of her baby boy and acknowledge and trust that she has raised a good man.

The ceremony takes place in the late spring while snow is still on the ground and the nights are cold. The mom makes a blanket for her son in preparation for his quest. As well, the elder and the young man meet regularly before the ceremony to talk about traditional values and ceremonies in the modern world and how to apply them.

The quest begins early in the morning with the boys lined up facing west. Behind the young men (who are usually between 12 and 14 years old) the moms stand in a line facing their sons' backs. The young men can hear their mothers crying and want to turn around, but know this is not the time and that their moms will get the community's support while they are gone. The elder men walk over to the moms to receive the blankets, then give the blankets to each boy. At this point, the young men are allowed to look back one more time at their mothers. When the boys turn, the moms also turn and start to walk away.

At this point, each boy is instructed to not return to the community until he has his spiritual name and his unique song. When he gets those, he is to make his way home, and share them with the community. He is not allowed food or water during this time, and the only additional clothing to protect him physically and spiritually out in the cold forest is the blanket his mom made him.

Some boys return almost immediately. Sometimes they are not ready, and there is no shame in that. They will get an opportunity each year until they are successful. Those who endure and receive the gifts of a name and song are received back home with hugs and handshakes. The whole community stops what it's doing and turns out to celebrate as each boy returns from the forest to share his name and his song. Then, for the man who was once a boy, there's a big caribou or moose meal, a warm shower, and a good night's sleep.

Oh, what a different world we would live in today if such ceremonies were readily available to us! We can only pray that it might someday soon be so. In the meantime, we must each do what we can to honor life and each other in such a way that our hearts and minds open to receive such a blessing. *Sookgapbii.* (It is good.)

The Gift

There are no specific ceremonies for recognizing children with psychic abilities. But here are a few suggestions that I wish someone had passed along to my own parents:

1. Respect the validity of what your children are saying. Yes, kids have very vivid imaginations and try to get attention however they can. But you'll know when your children are telling the truth by the despair in their voices, the sweat on their foreheads, and their racing hearts.

2. Educate yourself. If you have a child with psychic tendencies, read the literature, and watch movies available in any good New Age section at the bookstore or online.

3. Reassure your children they are not weird or crazy. Talk with other family members who might have similar experiences to share.

4. See a paranormal counselor, or someone who has worked with kids who have gifts. If possible, attend as a family to show your support.

5. One of the most healing things to do is reach out to others through sharing stories or joining a support group. The awareness of others with similar life experiences will help you—and your gifted children—feel more at ease.

SECTION II
Bridging Old and New

CHAPTER 6

Lori Morrison is an inspirationalist, an author, and a mystic. After a rare spiritual awakening, Lori vigorously studied sacred science, shamanic healing and quantum theory at the Foundation for Shamanic Studies, Four Winds Society, and the Casa K'in Maya Cosmic Institute. From the board rooms of Wall Street to the jungles of Central America, her unique experiences and alchemical formulas for life form the foundation of a successful consulting practice where her clients are leaping from the *ordinary* into the extraordinary. Initiated for two years as a "lightening shaman" by Mayan ancestral spirits, she facilitates personal transformation by helping people dissect their human experience and break through the cosmic veil that leads to higher levels of consciousness. She is the author of the award-winning book *Lori: The Disintegration of My Ordinary Reality*. She lives in Sedona, Arizona with her dog Gracie and cat Tut. When she is not planting seeds of awakening in others through her private practice, she enjoys chunks of Valrhona Chocolate, the smell of sweet sage, collecting crystals and stones, kicking fear in the butt, remaining curious, and hoping that friendly aliens choose to land in her backyard.

She can be reached at www.lorimorrison.com

A Mayan Initiation

As a young child I could see and speak with the spirit world. In my innocence, I thought that everyone could. This perception started to shatter when I realized that no one around me could see or relate to the multi-dimensional world I lived in. I withdrew from family and spent a lot of time in my bedroom where I could hang out with my spirit guides, watching and listening to them with great love and curiosity. Time went by, and the more I saw that I was different, the more desperate I became to conform. It was important to be liked and understood. My connections to the spirit world began to wither.

Born into a conservative and well-known family with deep roots in the lumber industry in Washington state. I lived an advantaged life that whisked me into the right university that led me to a powerful job in finance and into the arms of prominent men, jet setting around the world. My first major trauma arrived only three years into my first marriage when my first husband shot and killed himself. My second husband, who took me to El Salvador to live, died in my arms from a sudden stroke after a twenty-three-year marriage.

At age 51, I found myself alone, living among 80 acres of jungle on the edge of Lake Ilopango in El Salvador. It was a rough year after losing my husband, Tino. I loved our paradise that had been our home for over 20 years. Then, one day I stepped out on the lawn in front of the house, when a tiny random cloud appeared and rained on me. My household staff and I stared at each other in disbelief. Little did I know that this little cloud burst would be the start of a dramatic shamanic initiation.

A few days later, the evening before my 52nd birthday, there were electrical storms and the energy was shifting around my property. I began to hear the voices of ancient Mayan spirits in a language that I oddly understood. Then, the curtain of separation between my reality and the mystical world dropped and I was staring at a multitude of Mayan villages around me, watching smoke from their fires slither out of the small huts. The smell of copal seeped into my ever-expanding sensory awareness. I rubbed my eyes several times, wondering how I could see the past and still be aware of the present!

These same voices told me to walk to the end of the narrow peninsula in front of my house and lie down on the grass. I did so and was shifting into a deep trance—still aware as a circle of Mayan elders formed around me. My body began to disintegrate as I was hit by a beam of light, catapulting me into what would become the first of seven out-of-body experiences. After three hours I awoke, completely paralyzed. Eventually my senses returned and I was able to stagger back to my house. I had been infused with a massive amount of energy during this event and it flowed uncontrollably throughout my body. In shamanic societies, those who have this type of experience are called "lightening shamans" and go on to become some of the most powerful healers. It was a role I had no idea was waiting for me.

As I gazed around me, all the lights I saw were triangles—I was seeing the world through a lens of sacred geometry. Everything was connected. Everything. Trees, rocks, and plants were very alive and interacting with me. It felt like I'd been downloaded with a natural understanding of plant medicine, crystal and mineral energies. I could also access the spiritual hard drive of every person I would focus on. I could see illnesses inside their bodies and identify where their traumas were stored.

I barely knew what dimension I was in.

The night after I was struck by light I had absolutely no normal reference point or guide, just the voices and visions filling my mind. I wandered through my house, listening to them explain the energetic history of everything and everyone around me, funneling energetic "jolts" to confirm when I understood something. Unfortunately, these beings weren't very good at determining the appropriate levels of energy to hit me with. Their higher frequencies got so intense and I became so incredibly sensitive to frequencies that, in a fit of survival, I threw every electronic device I could find in my home into the swimming pool. The only thing that remained was a big-screen TV I couldn't detach from the wall.

As the days and weeks passed, I realized I'd become a revolving door to spirits, both negative and positive. Many overtook me, taking me to the dark crevices of my soul. My own fear drew other negative beings in. I saw shocking visions I could not explain—the pain and suffering of my past lives, the roles my friends and family had played in those lifetimes. I saw my many deaths and births like a cosmic play. It became so horrific, eventually I begged them to let me take my life. But they sabotaged every effort until I eventually gave up.

On the flip side, with the help of the Mayan spirits, I could easily travel to the depths of varying dimensions, to other planets and to meet strange beings. I would walk under the lake outside my home among a very large community of Mayans who had been living there for centuries. The most impressive experience was traveling deep inside the Milky Way. Here I was shown what they called God—a pulsating, cosmic drumbeat that was resonating at the same vibration as my own heartbeat. God was me—God was everyone— existing in our hearts that are driven by a constant sound that never stops penetrating the universe.

I also began to notice bruises on my arms and legs. "Where are they coming from?" I asked the spirits. They showed my ethereal body coming through the wall of my home after traveling to the bottom of the lake during my dream state. The reason I was sustaining injuries was sometimes the cells in my body were holding an awareness of me in physical human form while coming through the wall. As a result, that part of the body would be bruised.

Needless to say, all that was happening to me fractured my humanness to a point that I could not function as a normal human being. I was possessed, caught in another dimension, being introduced to more power than was good for me without more and better knowledge. Getting a handle on my new life was like being given a chain saw and told to cut a toothpick.

Like most shamans, I had been called and apparently there was nothing I could negotiate about it. I had been chosen by this group of Mayan spirits because of a karmic contract with them from my past. Not stepping on the path that had been set out for me, I was told, would lead to serious illness or death. Like it or not (and I did not like it!) these spirits were now the determining factor of my existence. Unfortunately, the Mayan spirits weren't the only ones I had to deal with.

Integration

On a friend's recommendation I finally decided to go to Colombia, South America, for a shamanic healing. A woman named Farides, the head witch, and Oscar, her star protégé, would put me back together. I started out with a lot of hope, submerging myself into an underground world of practicing brujos and brujas.

Throughout seven ceremonies they tried to remove the snarling spirits from my energy field. I sat amidst their black and white candles with my name written on them, watching them watching me, smoking cigars, intently scrutinizing the movement of the smoke and the color of ashes to determine the extent of spiritual damage I had endured by the invasion of spirits into my body.

One night I was draped in white gauze while several *brujos* blew smoke at me from cigars and used a nearby bonfire to blow up spirits that had invaded me. Another night I was taken to an altar where bottles of potions and plant medicines were mixed in buckets of water, then dumped on my body, drenching me in an assortment of essences meant to take away the stench of negative energies. Bucket after bucket of potions came splashing over me in the hope that my mind and clarity would return. Helping spirits merged into the body of Oscar, scolding me about my ego and how my mind was void of reverence and respect for the spirit world, until finally my ego was destroyed and

I was on my knees, begging for my sanity back.

Destruction of ego, beliefs, doubts and fears was the only option I had to survive. After a couple weeks I was finally able to go home when a clove of garlic rose to the top of a glass of water, proving that I was healed. The old me was gone. Even more telling than the garlic was the fact that when I looked into the mirror I no longer saw myself, but rather the face of a Mayan woman who had lived centuries ago. All agreed, it was a miracle I was spared.

Oscar, the shaman who worked so diligently to save me, died shortly after the work he did, making the ultimate sacrifice for reestablishing my wellbeing. I am indebted to him for my life and he is now a powerful spirit guide who works with me to this day.

I went back to the United States, hoping it was all over.

Far from it. Although I was no longer "possessed," I was still left with the problem of being unable to identify the energies and voices still engaging with me. I could as easily get thrown into darkness as I could receive energies of light and divine guidance that would lift me to transcendent states. It was a psychically and psychologically dangerous time. Many shamans do not make it past this point, ending up diagnosed with a multitude of psychic disorders, medicated and unable to function. I was walking a thin line between normal and insane.

I was attacked again—this time by spirits bent on having me kill myself as retribution for things I had done to defy Catholic teachings in a past lifetime in Spain. Although I was alone at the time, I felt a hand on the back of my head which then smashed my face onto a burning stove. I was pushed into a swimming pool and almost drowned. I was instructed to stage a suicide and kill myself. Not surprisingly, these circumstances ended with me in a mental hospital, deep on my way into the labyrinth of the mental health system with few options to ever get out.

Inside the hospital, benevolent spirits arrived to help me with the elimination of my fears, the most difficult task of my entire healing process. They told me that once I had cleared myself of any doubt, once I had finally reached the point of knowing the difference between good and evil, I would be ready to work for the highest good and become a healer.

Everything became a lesson, the food I ate, the hundreds of hours of downloads of information that showed me a behind-the-scenes view of the world. Everything that was happening to me was being done to destroy the beliefs that had been engraved on my psyche—hard-wired into my brain by social conditioning. Now, sitting in the ward, watching TV, I could not understand the commentary. All I could see were the subliminal messages and the submission of human minds to forces that were trying to control our perception of everything in order to mold us into collective conflict. It was beyond shocking.

I no longer believe much of what I hear in the media.

The training was not a course in spiritual growth, it was destruction of the self so that something much greater than a human could be funneled through me as a clear and purified vessel of healing. Eventually, the spirits taught me how to heal the mentally ill, how to walk through the hallways of the mental ward with powerful intention to heal the minds and souls of those there. Healing them, I healed myself. To my deep delight, many who were incarcerated were able to leave. And then I, too, was finally released.

A Long-due Ceremony

Returning to El Salvador, I was informed I had been chosen to be the human counterpart helping to perform a ceremony the Mayan spirits had been planning for hundreds of years that would release the multitude of souls that were living under the lake. This ceremony would take place on December 21st, 2012 at 4:00 a.m. in the morning. The invitation to meet my karma had arrived.

I prepared a massive bonfire at the same spot I had been hit by light. Early that morning on the appointed day, I carefully helped my Mayan guides open a portal which the spirits under the lake could move through. Beating the skin of my buffalo drum, my resonance—my energy essence—was that of the Mayan woman I had seen in the mirror that day before leaving Columbia. It penetrated the waters of the lake, and when it did, almost half a million souls left through the portal. It was a big success and pleased the spirits very much.

I definitely felt that my work was complete.

It wasn't.

The first person who came to me had been told to find a shaman by his psychiatrist. We met "by chance" on his way home from the appointment! I went to his home and found that both it and he were full of negative energies. I listened carefully to the instructions from the spirit world—where to apply myself as they worked through my eyes, ears, hands, energy centers and nervous system. Using rattles, specially-designed potions, divination practices and my willingness to allow what was needed to flow through me, one by one I removed the beings that had moved in. I did precisely what I was told, never wavering, and he was healed. He now lives a remarkable life.

I never told anyone I was a healer. But day after day, random people would find me, believing I could help them. I learned the roadways of the body's energetic system, popped synapses that were not firing in the brain, and learned how to connect the universal energy that flows between the mind and body, helping to restore wholeness.

I learned that the heaviness of words spoken in anger are stored in tissues and keep vibrating in eardrums. I would suck them out of people's bodies, providing relief from past traumas and hurts. I realized that negative thoughts were like vials of poison placed in an ethereal IV drip, creating disease.

The spirits taught me everything I needed to know at the moment I needed it. I would often be told to walk into a crystal store and be lead to a particular stone to purchase. It might sit on my shelf for a month until one day a patient would come and it would be the precise instrument I needed to heal them. Nothing was left to chance from the spirit perspective. Deer's tongue, sacred tobacco, obsidian, chunks of copal, bowls of sage, feathers, rosaries, old beads, water from sacred volcanos and Balinese springs stored in bottles alongside Florida water and sticks of Palo Santo became the makings of a spiritual medicine cabinet.

One of the more dramatic healings I've been involved with was for a woman, an ex-nun. She came to me with a heaviness and sense of burden that had her walking slumped over. She was covered in energies of scarcity and totally lacked any sense of connection to who she really was. As I began to open up my channels for guidance, much to my surprise, an enveloping energy came in, stronger than anything I had ever felt before. It was the energetic ID of Christ.

Massive emotions came over me and tears started flowing as my body attempted to release the intense energy coming through me. I told her that Christ was present in the room with us and she felt the energy as well. "He's telling me he's come to break the bonds of the sacred vows you've taken of poverty, chastity, and obedience," I said. "This will release you to live a better life."

Christ then cut the cords of bondage she had bound herself with. He then asked me to accompany her home, which I did. Once there, he guided me to a rosary she had worn as a nun and said she must take it to her back yard and lay it in a circle on the ground. She was to leave it there until there were further instructions from me.

Spring arrived and she called me with a voice filled with amazement. "Lori!" she cried, "The rosary is now a circle of flowers!"

Turns out the beads had been seeds and when they opened the roots escaped into the rich soil and had sprouted. At that moment a strong energy flew into my presence saying, "She is re-born. She is now free. The shackles put on her by her vows are released and she now has the opportunity to replenish what was missing."

Another case that made me feel so very good was an autistic child who was brought to me by his parents. "Josh" (not his real name) was fractured between the third and fourth dimensions, unable to successfully be in either one. In addition, his diet and supplements were affecting his mind. I worked with him once, teaching him how to journey and connect to his spirit guides so he could better understand the worlds he lives in. Now, he journeys and enjoys this world and reality while being able to distinguish between it and the next dimension. He's also learning how to move about the universe. The results were nothing short of amazing.

The stories continue as each time the spirits come, work their magic through me and the blessings remain. It is not easy doing this kind of work in this world. I have been called a witch, an atheist, schizophrenic, bipolar, sick, devil worshipper, and possessed by people trying to paint me into the darkness of fear.

Of course, none of that defines what I have become. The darkness serves a purpose. You cannot know the light without the dark, nor help others to remove negative forces if you have never experienced them. As much as I sometimes wish for a day of ignorance to all that has happened, I know that I must embrace my purpose and serve the spirit world. My life was never about me anyway, it was about how I would show up in the world.

The Gift

My journey has given me great hope and an entirely different view of those who have been marginalized and discarded in our world, many corralled into a broken health system with inadequate references for their treatment. My dream come true would be for mental health professionals to work hand-in-hand with shamans who have had significant awakenings into their craft and are now stabilized with extraordinary intuitive skills. Combining the knowledge of these modern shamans with traditional therapists on the front line of the health crisis in our world would lead to dramatic shifts in the possibilities of recovery. Instead of telling people that they have an incurable disease and need medications for the rest of their lives, we could give them assurances and tools that have the power to change their health and their entire life's outcome.

There is so much we can learn from both sides of the spectrum. The shaman seeks balance among all things, the plant spirits, the winged ones, the swimmers, the creepy crawlers, the four-legged and the two-legged, by trying to integrate their energies into a collective, taking advantage of the gifts that each brings to wholeness. Reconnecting people to the spiritual and natural world, coupled with the knowledge of anatomy, disease, pathology, natural medicines, psychology, technology and the quantum world would be a most powerful health system and a great contribution to humanity. I know this for a fact, because I currently work with both paradigms.

To me, a human being looks like is a disco ball. All the aspects of their human life are small mirrors, each one a microcosm that reflects the reality that is being created from their interior thought/emotional world. A healthy person's mirrors are shining, reflecting a healthy mind and soul that is flourishing on life's journey. Layers of unhealthy conditioning and misperceptions become blemishes on the mirrors, creating a dusty appearance, obscuring the person's core light, diminishing them. If this continues, their light deteriorates, the disco ball stops spinning, the inner destruction begins, and they begin to pull more negativity and dis-ease to them.

With the help of a sophisticated computer program/encyclopedia of almost 200,000 vibrational remedies, contraindications, formulas and holistic protocols, I can throw these healing frequencies onto the "disco ball" of the holographic self — the patient who has come to me — discovering exactly what supplements, toxins, protocols, sensitivities and solutions resonate with the individual, providing a guide book and intuitive path into what the person needs for life optimization on a multitude of levels.

This holistic and non-invasive approach—this blend of ancient and new healing—can unravel years and years of detrimental thinking and lifestyle and put a person on the path to uncovering the root of their illnesses, guiding them into therapeutic solutions that help to uncover the healthy lifestyle waiting for them.

The possibilities are endless. We just have to be open to them.

Practice

The Mayans have termed this moment as the time that humanity enters the great hall of mirrors. When you wake up in the morning, take a few minutes and use your mirror as a tool of honest self-reflection. We all must face our behaviors to find the promised land of change. Our divine connection exists on the other side of fear. By tapping into source, or Hunab Ku as the Mayan termed it, we will find that which vibrates through our universal hearts, and then we will feast on all that feeds the soul.

CHAPTER 7

Jan Engels-Smith is an author, a Shamanic Practitioner (ShD) a Tibetan, Usui, and Karuna Reiki Master, a Licensed Professional Counselor, a Chemical Dependency Specialist and a Hypnotherapist. Jan's mission is to provide excellence in shamanic education and to support personal growth for well-being, adapting ancient healing techniques to contemporary life in the 21st century. An expert in her field, she personally has performed 3500 shamanic soul retrievals.

In 1994, Jan founded LightSong School of 21st Century Shamanism and Energy Medicine, developing the first energy medicine curriculum of its kind, supporting those with a curious interest in energy medicine right through to those who would like to obtain a doctorate in shamanism. (Sh.D.) Jan has written two books: *Through the Rabbit Hole: Exploring Energy and the Shamanic Journey* and *Becoming Yourself: The Journey from Head to Heart,* which won the Reader's Choice Award. She is a featured author in *Shamanic Transformation: True Stories of the Moment of Awakening*, writes a monthly article for Sedona *Journal of Emergence* and has authored two CDs: *Take Your Body With You* a shamanic drumming CD, and *Awaken~Unburden~Create,* a meditation CD package of shamanic principles.

To contact Jan: wwwlightsong.net

Teaching Shamanism in the 21st Century

Years ago, a strong message came through to me from the spirits. It unfolded through a series of daily journeys in a month's time. The simplified but powerful conclusion to the message was, "Don't ever think you know anything, because as soon as you think that you know or have the answer you have just prevented us from teaching you." Often, I will ask the spirits to reveal something to me that I have missed in my interpretation. I instill this inquisitive, unlimited possibility curiosity in my students. I also tell them that just because the spirits teach you something doesn't mean there isn't more to learn about the topic. Stay open and inquisitive with your questions. Stay away from spiritual arrogance.

The beginnings of my connection with shamanism began some years before I even knew what a shaman was. My husband and I were living in Dallas, Texas with three small children and I had an active practice as a professional counselor, generally using traditional psychological approaches to working with clients who suffered from the generic problems of depression, doubts of self-worth, inordinate fears, and all the other conditions common to our industrial society. I also worked in the dissociate ward in a local psychiatric hospital. Many of these clients suffered from multiple personality disorder, frequently brought on from a history of satanic ritualistic abuse. I was affected emotionally by the horrors they had encountered. I regularly felt stretched thin by the expressed terrors, the complexity of their reality and my desire to bring them relief. I had success with many clients, but I was far from satisfied. I also developed an awe for mystical, unexplainable realities with which that I had no personal familiarity, while witnessing daily physical and sensational transformations in front of my eyes.

The experience that changed all that was a vision I had of an old Native American woman who materialized in my living room. I walked into the room and she was standing there. I was surprised and a bit alarmed. When I approached her and asked who she was, she replied:

I am you,

I am your mother,

I am your sister,

I am your grandmother,

I am the Earth.

She had gray hair pulled back tightly in a bun, and her skin was wrinkled and weathered by life. She was wrapped in a wool blanket and smoking a pipe. She asked if I wanted to join in the sisterhood, but warned me that my life would be forever changed. I was dreadfully fearful, perplexed and alarmed with her presence, but a crow outside my living room window kept cawing and with each caw I heard the word "trust." I nodded my head and replied, "Yes."

I remember being extremely nervous, but there was a peculiar kind of strength surrounding and supporting me. We sat down and she handed me the pipe and we smoked it together, passing it back and forth. When we finished smoking the pipe, she spoke again. "Your guidance will be provided. Your medicine that you carry is North: Wisdom, Healing, and Love. Begin now to learn to understand the Ways." I turned away, responding to a sound behind me, thinking someone else had walked into the room. When I turned back, the old woman was gone.

The apparition left me bewildered, confused and concerned for my own mental health. The vision, coupled with my experiences in the psych ward, had me doubting what I thought of as reality. My friends, family and Sunday school class thought that the stress of my work was affecting me. Many reacted to my story with alarm and concern for my mental state. Longtime friends deserted me and I began to feel isolated, judged, and unheard.

The more I tried to defend and explain my experience, the crazier I sounded. It was years before I would fully understand what was being communicated to me. At the time, I did not understand even the concept of visions—much less the idea of medicine, apparitions, pipes, "ways" or spirits from another realm. I had been seeking meaning for my life beyond the traditional field of counseling and I sought better solutions for my clients who suffered such loss and pain. My decision to say "Yes" to the mystery and to trust in the message would redirect my life in ways that I could never have imagined. But in the meantime I was clueless as to what to study. What were "the ways" she mentioned?

And then I had a dream of a voice that spoke from a black void. The voice told me to move to the Pacific Northwest. I had no idea who or what spoke to me. But the message was clear, short, and direct and felt like a reprieve from the loss and judgment I was experiencing. Through a series of spirit-led, synchronistic events, our family was able to move within the year.

Soon after the move to Portland, Oregon, I encountered a person who channeled angels. During a session with this channel, I finally received an explanation of my vision and direction. "This is your life," she said, handing me a book on a shamanic healing practice called soul retrieval. I read the book with great anticipation and the material had a strange familiarity. At times it felt like I had written the material and even knew what the next sentence was going to say.

At the same time, I also experienced my first sweat lodge. While there, the "pourer" of the lodge asked me to assist a native elder in the Lakota tribe, getting him to various speaking engagements presenting native elder wisdom. I ended up having to accommodate him and about seven other family members. I even had to change my attire to fit his needs. (I usually wore pants and needed to wear a skirt to be in his presence.) He fondly ended up calling me his servant girl, inviting me and my family to come and visit him at his home, complimenting me on my willingness and patience with his ordering me around. At that point he asked me to attend gatherings at his house, and I sensed I had passed some sort of personalized test.

This was the beginning of my preparation to learn The Ways. From 1992 to this day, I participated with this Lakota Native-American tribe. There was no formal training on how to contact Spirit. But I learned much of their ways, as well as how to be polite, willing, devoted and curious—all necessary attributes helping me to surrender to Spirit as I later learned the healing ways of shamanism.

My first official training in shamanism occurred in 1992, with Michael Harner, the founder of the

Foundation of Shamanic Studies. There I learned about the organization of the different worlds a shaman works within and the shamanic tools of drumming, rattling, journeying, and other healing techniques. I trained in depossession with Betsy Bergstrom and studied soul retrieval with Sandra Ingerman. Soul retrieval is a shamanic technique where a person who has splintered off parts of their soul because of abuse and trauma is guided to find and restore these lost parts of themselves. It is believed that soul retrieval is the oldest known healing procedure on the planet. Since training with Sandra and then becoming her assistant for a workshop, I have performed over 3,500 soul retrievals. And every soul retrieval I did (or helped the spirits with) I learned from the spirits vast amounts of information about life, other lifetimes, karma, the power of words, human energetic systems, energy matrixes, thought forms, empowerment/disempowerment, self-care, wellness, the death process, discarnate beings, the value of relationships, the evolution of humanity, and why we incarnate in the first place. The spirits also offered new insights and remedies to crippling contemporary problems such as anxiety, and depression.

One of the soul retrievals that had a profound effect on me involved a young girl who suffered from night terrors. Night terrors are different from nightmares in that the people experiencing them can't be awakened. In fact, the more you try to awaken them, the deeper they travel into their terror. Often the sleeping person makes bone chilling, eerie sounds. The sleeping person may have eyes open or closed. If open, you can see soul-deep the horror of their experience.

The young girl's mother had attempted to find healing in other ways, including medication, but nothing had been successful. The journey I embarked on to find relief for this child brought not only healing for her but also an experience for me that influenced my confidence and surety of the power of the shamanic ways, bringing a deeper understanding of the complexity of life and the importance of journeying to other lifetimes.

During this journey, I had a vision of an African scene involving an African warrior. He was very short, dressed in stereotypical dress that was probably sourced from images I had seen in *National Geographic Magazine*, and carrying a spear. He wore a black mask with grass hair. As he approached me he was screaming in what I assumed was an African language, waving his hands and spear and stomping his feet. I had no idea what he was saying, but he was obviously angry and threatening. I felt as though I needed the protection of my spirit allies and I called on my power animals to help me understand. They told me the girl's night terrors were the result of a black magic curse placed on her soul in another lifetime.

I was perplexed on how to respond to this, but I received instructions from my spirit allies and following their direction I was able to break the spell. I don't remember the instructions except they were very basic, say this, blah, blah, blah and wave your hand this way, nothing like the techniques I use today. However, they did the trick. The little African warrior dropped his spear, deflated to a fraction of his size, and walked away in a powerless, defeated way. After breaking the spell, I continued with the journey to bring back any lost soul parts.

There had been much soul loss and loss of power within my client because of the night terrors. The spirits made sure that all was in order before we left the journey.

After completing the soul retrieval, I spent time explaining to both my client and her mother what had happened during the journey. We then discussed the recommendations given to me by the spirits about how to facilitate her healing by calling in certain healing allies at night before bed. With this advice, the mother and daughter left my office.

Now, my normal procedure after a session is to clean with sage the sacred items I had used during the soul retrieval. As I was doing this, I heard a loud crash in an adjoining room. A strange energy surged within me and I ran to see what had happened. On the floor lay an African mask that had fallen off the wall. I stared in both disbelief and amusement, the fear that had momentarily surged through my body melting away. There was a real similarity between the mask that hung on my wall and the one I encountered in the journey, and I realized this mask had not accidentally fallen off the wall, but had, more than likely, jumped off the wall to get my attention. I laughed out loud as I picked up the mask, realizing how blatant the spirits can be getting your attention.

From my work I've learned about the "realness" of spirits, how they can physically come into a space, touch you, do healings, move objects and sometimes people, how rattles can fly, drums can fly and how things that Westerners would label paranormal are actually "normal" occurrences once we give Spirit the room to create healing miracles.

So, I took the mask into my office and did a journey with it, asking, "What do you know about this black magic stuff I just encountered?" During the journey the mask gave me all kinds of information about spells, curses, the power of the spoken word, how to move energy to counter spells, and how to become invisible when I get myself into dangerous situations during a journey. In fact, it told me to wear it when I needed to become invisible in non-ordinary reality. I moved the mask into my office space and since then it has become a beloved ally in the spiritual realms.

At that point I walked out of my office and felt compelled to turn on the TV and watch Oprah. To my amazement, the topic of her program that day was night terrors. She had several guests discussing the topic, including doctors and patients. The doctors were stating they had no cure for night terrors nor did they understand what created them. Their treatment was drug related which had many side effects, especially on the quality of life for their patients. Patients described the horrors of night terrors. Parents or spouses that were witness to the night terrors expressed the same type of horror. The entire program was focused on the reality of these episodes for people and the fact that there is no cure that medical science has discovered.

In my story of the young girl's night terrors, I believe that there is a blatant and clear message from the spirits that in order to help people with night terrors we must look in the direction of curses from other lifetimes. Modern methods to help those that suffer from this affliction don't work and can cause more harm. The spirits, in their unconditional and unrelenting efforts to bring us messages of wellbeing, used this soul retrieval and the topic of Oprah's show to bring this information through to me.

Another soul retrieval I would like to share showed me the intricacy of the profound multidimensionality of the "reality" we are living within. During the session, as I entered into my altered shamanic state of consciousness, I could hear drumming off in the distance and felt myself being drawn to the sound. This was not the drumming I was listening to on my headset that I use in journeying, but a drumming off in the distance—faint yet inviting.

I felt myself being drawn to the sound as though the Pied Piper was hypnotizing me and I automatically followed. I journeyed seemingly very far away and found myself energetically entering a room where a shaman stood, calling, whistling, and drumming to her allies, beseeching them to come to her in order to aid a client lying on the floor. The feeling of love was all encompassing, surpassing what I have ever experienced in physical form. I had "become" compassion, love, and grace as I merged into this shaman from another dimension and time. I realized I was the spiritual ally she was calling to for aid. This other shaman's client and my client were the same soul in two different lifetime expressions. The other lifetime I was encountering was the one that needed to be healed in order for "my" client to heal. As if that information wasn't profound enough, I also realized that I was the spirit ally being called in for the healing.

This soul retrieval affected me deeply. Not only can we tap into other physical lives of ourselves, we can access our existences as spirit ancestors and allies *between* physical incarnations. The multidimensional aspects of the soul are mind blowing and something logic can't comprehend. We have these rich, full expressions of ourselves outside of being physical, and the spirits can direct the shaman into other dimensions and create multidimensional healings. Since that particular journey, I've realized that shamans must not be limited by what they think they know, including how to perform a particular ceremony, because that just creates a limitation in information that wants to come through, keeping us from new, unexplored solutions to modern problems and expansions in the world of healing.

A Quantum Shift and the Founding of LightSong

Our indigenous elders taught that the relationship between shaman and Spirit is an intimate and honored connection. The shaman trusts that the spirits will work through each person to bring healing and the spirits trust the shaman to bring healing methods to the physical world. But this work is a never-ending evolution.

Over the years, I began to see limitations with many traditional shamanic practices as they were being applied to modern ailments and peoples. Ancient shamanism lacks the ability to empower the client. It also lacks the follow-through that sustains the individual's growth and lifelong attention to becoming one's true divine self. This is through no fault of the practitioners. It's just that in ancient shamanism, tribal members were raised believing in the spiritual realms and in the traditions of the rites and practices of the shaman.

They were aligned with accepting the medicine man or woman as the authority in matters of healing and the spirit. Today, our modern culture believes in doctors trained in Newtonian physics who compartmentalize the body, treating it like a soulless machine whose parts need fixing. The doctors don't believe in Spirit, so we don't believe in Spirit. They believe in drugs and surgery, so we believe in drugs and surgery. We have a "prove-it-to-me" scientific mentality that resists easy acceptance of things that are novel or out of the mainstream of collective thought.

And yet quantum theory has also come along, giving us a new scientific view of life as an infinite set of interdependent energy systems interacting in a dynamic holographic information-based universe, a view quite similar to the world that shamans have been working within for thousands of years. Another big shift in perception has been brought about by the New Age movement which has introduced humanity to the understanding that not only do we have a divine connection, but *we are divine.* The power base has shifted and we are transitioning from a dependence upon outer authority to an inner authority where we will no longer require the intercession of either priests or shamans to access the spirit world/universe that lies within us.

A person who struggles with problems in life is one who has not yet come to grips with his/her existence, not just as a part of the universe, but as the universe itself. Each one of us is a field of energy that desires to recognize our oneness with the cosmos. It has been through witnessing the spirits' approach to healing, humanity, love, and compassion that I came to see the universe as a fully integrated field of energy that is perfect in design and of which we are both a reflection and at one. I decided my mission in life would be to not simply achieve personal healing while working as a healer for others, but to find a way for greater numbers of people in this modern age of fragmentation and lost souls to master a modern form of shamanic practice that could support dramatic change in the 21^{sst} century.

Modern shamanism must address the whole person by engaging the individual in their own healing and thus their self-empowerment and evolution. To that end I founded the *LightSong School of 21st Century Shamanism and Energy Medicine* for the express purpose of providing a different approach to healing and personal growth. We have an accredited teaching program that includes bachelors, master and doctorate level programs that has attracted thousands of people to a new healing exploration that involves continued connections to teachers, assistants, and fellow travelers on the spiritual path.

Modern shamanism must be based on collaboration, support, love, and unity—the corner posts of the New Earth we wish to evolve into. In the old shamanic traditions there was often a lot of rigidity, fear, and bids for power. And yet, the universe is sustained and honored by the ways in which we express our love. The spirits understand this and are often puzzled by the failure of humans to realize the power of something so simple. Fundamental to the new healing approach is the recognition that our interactions cannot be based on mechanisms, structures, and processes alone, but must be grounded in a sincere and loving environment where every action is guided by the desire to serve and to be available in person and spirit, that healing and building connections are first and foremost about caring and love.

Everyone in the program is on a continuing path of growing and becoming one's true self—the perfect being that the universe created. They learn that, as fields of energy, we project vibrations that affect all other things in the universe and that the energy we send out in our thoughts, actions, and words returns to us in a like form. They come to understand that when we project negative vibrations, we attract negative consequences and inhibit our capacity for healing and transformation. As well, they learn that the recognition and embodiment of our brilliance projects waves of positive energy that change everything around us, returning in positive ways that enhance our souls while creating a better world.

The first effort of new initiates in the school is to learn to love themselves—for we cannot truly express our love for others until we have seen and accepted our own worthiness. Self-examination, meditation, quieting the mind, presence, mindfulness, and conscious listening are integral parts of the program. We also have established mentoring programs. From the very first class, students have access to and receive guidance from volunteer assistants who listen, guide, advise, support, and redirect. In receiving this support, they learn valuable mentoring skills that will serve them well if they choose to practice shamanic healing. The whole process builds trust, confidence, and community.

LightSong's masters and doctoral students are required to document their healing work and submit findings of "new" information, insights, and modalities that the spirits have brought through to enhance healing and assist the evolution of energy medicine, such as the insights I learned about cross-dimensional, multiple-lifetime healing from the soul retrieval stories I shared. As a result, we have a growing body of guidance dedicated to the advancement of shamanism as it evolves in this modern age.

A continuing expansion of one's consciousness and the personal growth that comes from a never-ending attention to one's own self-worth is the way of 21st century shamanism. There cannot be just an acceptance of the powers of the spiritual world, but a true understanding that emerges from the engagement with modern science and others in a common journey that reassures and validates the truth of the spiritual experience. A New Earth materializes when we collectively realize our unity in this mystical realm that we call the universe and we bring about the changes that heal us and our world.

The Gift

To aid you in your own self-evolution, a link is provided to a recording I constructed that will guide you in a beautiful, relaxing meditation to your true self. The true self is the version of you that is divinely perfect and is the full embodiment of your actualized potentials. You were born divine and contained within your being is the blueprint of divine perfection that has been hidden away by the perceived reality of human limitation. The intention is that you have a tool to use regularly, for it is the practice of the feeling of what the True Self feels like that will help you embody this version of yourself more regularly. Listen to this often and thrive! http://lightsong.net/true-self-meditation/

CHAPTER 8

Robin Cathleen Coale, MA, LPC is a licensed psychotherapist, shamanic and energy healer, teacher, and clairvoyant with a private practice in Santa Fe, New Mexico. She offers counseling and shamanic and energy healing to clients in Santa Fe, and also does remote counseling and healing work with clients throughout the U.S., Europe, Asia and the Caribbean. Robin completed a three-year advanced shamanic training with Michael Harner and trainings in Soul Retrieval, Extraction, Healing with Light, and Medicine for the Earth with Sandra Ingerman. She is a certified teacher of shamanic courses from Sandra Ingerman. She has studied Dynamic Energetic Healing, Emotional Freedom Technique, Energy Medicine, Cognitive Behavioral Therapy, and Mindfulness Practices. Prior to her current work, Robin spent 16 years in California legislative politics as a contract lobbyist representing a wide range of interests, worked as the Director of Government Affairs for the Western United States for US Sprint, and Chief of Staff to the Minority Leader in the California State Assembly. Robin has an MA in Counseling from Southwestern College, Santa Fe, NM, and a BA in Inter-American Studies with a double major in Political Science and Public Administration from the University of the Pacific in Stockton, CA.

She can be reached at
http://www.sacredshamanichealing.com

Shamanism: The Missing Element In Our Health and Mental Health System

I never wanted or expected to be a healer or what some would call a "shaman." But destiny pounded on my door and I had no choice but to answer. I was working in California state legislative politics when my psychic sight began to open. I did not ask for it. I did not seek it out. I did not want it. What I began seeing and experiencing defied my imagination and all logical and rational thinking.

My first vision came when I was about 30-years old. I had just gone to bed when an angel with red hair and blue eyes appeared at the foot of my bed. I put my fingers up to both of my eyes and poked them, opening and closing them to make sure I was not asleep and dreaming. I was quite awake and she was definitely there. Then she disappeared. I did not give this any further thought until three weeks later when I was in Washington DC and walked into an art gallery in Georgetown. The first painting I saw was a red-headed angel with wings. I knew it was a sign from Spirit that what I had seen three weeks before was a real visitation and that I did not imagine it. I bought the painting and she still hangs in my bedroom.

It wasn't until several years later that my sight really opened up. Unfortunately, the things I began seeing were not all as pretty as the angel. While the spirit world is full of beautiful, benevolent and compassionate beings like angels, saints, nature spirits, gods and goddesses, it is also full of dark and malevolent energies that are actively working against light workers and the light. Seeing and experiencing dark energies was part of my shamanic initiation and exploration and ascent into my own power as a healer. But I had no understanding or framework for any of it.

My Initiation Starts

One day while sitting in meditation in my home in Sacramento, a Native American spirit approached me and gave me an amethyst crystal to place in my 3rd eye. Immediately after, I saw a black human-like form approach me. Then it went away. Years later I was told that dark forces may attack the 3rd eye to prevent people from psychically seeing and also try to make them go crazy. I was being protected by the Native American visitor. Not long after, I was alone in the house and was knocked down onto one knee from a standing position after being hit by a sharp blow to my left shoulder.

In the steam room at a local health club, a saint/ascended master I had never heard of appeared to me. There I was, naked, with sweat dripping down my body as he stood next to me talking. He gave me an etheric ring with a sacred symbol on it and I placed it on my finger as directed. The moment the ring went on, I heard an alarm resound throughout the etheric realms and immediately I was propelled into a vision/experience of running for my life through a jungle, being chased by people who wanted to kill me. Much later I understood that the alarm meant my light and power were activating in such a way as to cause alarms to go off, and that there were forces directly invested in making certain I would not be on board to do my light work.

From this point on I experienced frequent psychic attacks by forces I did not understand.

I thought I was experiencing the dark energies because I worked in the political arena. Thinking it might be a way to escape these energies and to leave behind work that was no longer fulfilling to me, I moved to Santa Fe, New Mexico with my husband and our nine-month old son.

No such luck. I spent the next 15 years battling energies that sought to harm me and my family. I was slammed to the ground while skiing, ending up with a bruised rib, black eye and a cut from my goggles when I hit the hard snow pack. No one was anywhere near me when it happened. I was pushed from behind when walking down my office stairs. Beings came into my dreams and bit me on the neck. I experienced poison sticks, like wooden shish kabob skewers, inserted into my throat. The next day my lymph glands were the size of large gum balls. My young son was pushed into a wall and later thrown down stairs, breaking his collarbone.

At times it was utterly mind bending and terrifying. There was no one to turn to for answers. I didn't have a teacher, mentor or guide to help me. I was a lone wolf and apparently this was my path. I remember a moment when I prayed to God to let me die if I wasn't provided a way to overcome the torments of the forces assaulting me. But throughout it all, I never questioned the validity of the visions and what I was seeing and experiencing. It was all very real.

Not all shamanic healers have to undergo initiations that involve fighting malevolent energies or traveling to the depths of darkness and despair that I did. It was not until many years later that I was told by told by a gifted seer in Europe that I had seven professional black magicians actively working against me. He said he'd never seen anything like it. I was dumbfounded. Why me? I didn't even know any dark magicians! The answers were to be revealed many years later when I worked with two different mediums who essentially told me the same thing. It seems I have been on the front lines of the battlefield with the archangels where there is an epic battle raging between the tremendous forces of dark versus the light. My soul had chosen to undertake this task.

Training

A couple of years after moving to Santa Fe, I went back to school to get a master's degree in counseling. One of the more interesting experiences that happened while I was in graduate school occurred as I was doing an exercise in class with a partner. I saw an energetic knife sticking out of his lower spine. I had never seen anything like this before. "Does your back hurt, by chance?" I asked him casually.

"It's killing me," he replied. "Why do you ask?"

I told him what I saw and then asked if anyone was angry with him. As it turned out, he and his girlfriend had had a big fight the day before. Even though I had no training in this sort of thing, I wanted to remove the knife and relieve him of the pain. So, I asked his permission to remove it. He agreed, and as soon as I pulled out the knife he told me the pain was gone.

When I graduated, I began a private counseling practice. Not long after I started, I began seeing my clients' energy bodies, the field of energy inside their bodies and sometimes around the body as well. I also started receiving information about them and would say things out of the blue, not knowing where or how I received the information.

After some time, I began asking a few of my clients if they would like an energy clearing, free of charge at the end of their session. The feedback I received was that they felt better and lighter afterwards, which was a good thing. However, I began to get sick because I was unknowingly taking on their energies.

It became clear that if I was going to allow the healing gifts to be expressed through me, I needed to have proper training. So, I enrolled in Michael Harner's three-year program in the study of advanced shamanism. (Harner, an anthropologist and the author of the classic book *The Way of the Shaman*, is hugely responsible for bringing shamanism back into the Western world.) Many of the journeys he required us to go on were shamanic initiations. For me, they were as natural as breathing. I had found home.

During my training with Harner, I discovered that, unbeknownst to me, I had come from a lineage of healers and seers. During a session he asked us to do a shamanic journey to meet a famous healer. Not knowing where to go, I asked my power ally to take me to whomever. I was taken to my great-grandmother from Lebanon whom I never knew. She told me she was a seer, bone knitter and midwife. I merged with her and could feel her large gnarly hands, the length of her neck, her strong back, as well as every muscle in her body.

Since that journey and meeting she has been a constant presence in my practice. Another ancestor, her daughter, (my deceased grandmother whom I knew as Situ), also from Lebanon, appeared to me one day while I was driving. She appeared directly above my steering wheel and said, "Your mother had the gift. I had the gift. Now it is time to pass it along to you. This is the gift from all the women in our lineage since the beginning of time."

Unconsciously I turned my palms face up on the steering wheel and immediately golden light started pouring into my palms. I asked her what the gift was and she said, "You'll find out." Then she vanished. It wasn't long after that I began to feel and "see" through my hands the energies and blockages present in my clients. I also became more clairvoyant.

I continued my studies with Sandra Ingerman, author of many books on shamanism, including the important book, *Soul Retrieval*. Her work and her teachings not only deepened and expanded the knowledge of shamanism in the Western world, but popularized it and made it more accessible. Afterwards, my learning continued as I was taught, guided, supported and protected on my shamanic path by beings on the other side, including ancestors, angels, ascended masters, gods/goddesses and power allies. Eventually I began to offer shamanic healing in my private practice.

Blending Shamanism and Psychology

Trauma experts and leaders in the field of energy psychology point out that in order to heal trauma the practitioner needs to employ healing modalities that access the right side of the brain. Shamanism is one of many such right-brain modalities, along with Eye Movement Desensitization and Reprocessing (EMDR), Emotional Freedom Technique (EFT), guided imagery and creative visualization, to name a few.

Despite this information, our current Western

system of healing still focuses on the physical, mental and emotional aspects of the human being, while failing to consider the soul or the spirit. As a result, even though we have great advances in medicine and technology, as a nation, we are sicker than ever.

Shamanism is the oldest form of spiritual healing on the planet and shamanic healing is a perfect complement to mental health therapy because it goes to places that traditional talk therapy cannot access. Shamans believe that all illness and disease have their root cause in a spiritual imbalance caused by soul loss, power loss, or the intrusion of unwanted energy. From my experience, I would add that these problems can also be attributed to ancestral patterns/obligations/commitments handed down through generations, incorrect, negative, self-defeating and sabotaging belief systems adopted by the individual and embedded in the body as truth, and past life traumas that are bleeding through into the present.

Shamanism is the missing element in our health and mental health system. It is not a replacement for therapy or medical attention, but rather, it should be woven into our health and mental health system as a key component for healing.

Over the years, my work has evolved and now encompasses both counseling and traditional shamanic healing techniques such as soul retrieval, power retrieval, extraction, divination, and psychopomp, (helping people who have passed on to make their way into the Light), energy healing, healing on the cellular level, ancestral healing, divine transmissions, clairvoyance and channeling. When a client comes to me for healing I tell them "I don't know anything. My only goal is to be a clear and open channel for Divine healing." My prayer is always to be an instrument for Spirit for the absolute highest healing of my clients.

Soul Retrieval/Past Life Healing/Energy Healing/Somatic Work

Soul retrieval is a key component of shamanic healing addressing the issue of soul loss. Everyone has soul loss, it is part of the nature and experience of being human and living on this Earth. Soul loss occurs when we have shock, pain, trauma or loss and it is the body's natural self-defense mechanism for handling the trauma. Some symptoms of soul loss include addiction, (as individuals attempt to fill the empty spaces inside where soul parts have left), depression, disassociation, and memory loss.

We all need healing for our torn and damaged souls and our weary spirits, and I believe everyone should have soul retrieval done as part of their medicine. I am continually impressed with how my clients benefit when soul parts are returned. Years ago, I worked with a client I will call Sam, who was referred to me by his therapist. He had had two mental breakdowns and a stay in rehab in the five years prior to seeing me. I did power retrieval and soul retrieval for him, returning three soul parts. One of the soul parts that left when he had one of his breakdowns told me he was "a broken man with a broken life."

Fortunately, returning soul parts do not come back in with the same trauma that triggered their leaving in the first place. On the contrary, they come in healed and whole, bringing a gift in the form of some assistance to help the client. I work primarily with the angelic ones to give the soul parts the necessary healing. Once healed, I dialogue with the soul part, asking what gift it brings back to my client in being reunited with him or her. This particular soul part said it would help heal Sam's heart and his life, bring back happiness and joy and help him find peace. He emailed me a few weeks later writing that he had "experienced joy for the first time in years."

Another client, who I'll call Susan, came to me for depression and anxiety. She said she'd done a lot of therapy but was searching for more healing. I had one session with her and did power retrieval and soul retrieval, retrieving three soul parts. One of the returning soul parts was four-years old and was bringing her the gift of helping her to be herself again and to be happy, playful and joyful. Three months after seeing her she wrote, "My whole life has just fallen into place...I found energy and enthusiasm again...I feel so happy and content right now. I wanted to let you know that I believe your work was the most helpful...."

Energy healing is also a part of my shamanic practice and the result of the gift of the transmission my grandmother gave to me. It is not uncommon for me to see an energetic imprint in a client's body that is a memory from the current life or an unconscious memory held from a past life. Our souls carry the memories of every lifetime we have ever had and our cells carry memory as well. For example, if a client has been physically abused, the area on his/her body will hold the memory of the violence.

Occasionally traumatic memories held from a past life bleed through into the current life. In some cases, there is a trigger that causes the past life memory to ignite. For example, I worked with a client who was pregnant with her second child. She came to me because she was having panic attacks (which she had never previously experienced) and was deathly afraid that something was going to happen to her and her baby.

I knew it was a past-life memory that was ignited when she became pregnant. In my shamanic journey for her, I was taken to a house in Ireland with a thatched roof where I saw my client pregnant, lying on the dirt floor of the cottage, ready to give birth. In that past life she was unable to deliver and she and the baby both died on that dirt floor, alone. The spirit of the baby from that lifetime was the spirit of the baby she was currently carrying. Her fear and her anxiety attacks were directly linked to this past-life memory and to this child. Healing her panic attacks required healing the trauma from that lifetime. This was done and my client's panic attacks and the fear that something would happen to her and her unborn baby went away completely after one session. She went on to deliver a healthy baby girl.

Sometimes there is no trigger, but there exists an imprint from a past life trauma that causes some disturbance with current life circumstances. One woman came in with problems with her ankles. I removed energetic shackles on her ankles held over from a past life where she was a slave. She also battled issues of domination and victimization in this life which were paralyzing her, making it difficult for her to move forward. I've also removed energetic ropes from around the necks of clients who died by hanging in previous lives. Not surprisingly, some of these clients had throat problems as well as difficulty speaking their truth and speaking in public. Phobias can often be traced to traumas in past lives which are bleeding through into current time.

Somatic work (working with the body) is an important part of my process with clients as the body holds information and memory which can assist greatly in the healing process. I assist clients in identifying areas of the body and aspects of themselves that are holding onto negative, limiting and sabotaging beliefs or untruths and releasing them. These beliefs may come from a parent, other family member, or be inherited through the genetic lineage. These false beliefs are like a virus in a computer, a negative program corrupting the entire system. For example, I have seen many cases where the oppressive and restrictive ideas about the role of women have flowed through lineages, making it difficult for some women to be in their power, stand up for themselves, and be self-confident. Through guided imagery I helped them locate and identify the negative belief, understand what age it was adopted, where it came from, and helped them release it from the body memory, thus allowing room for replacement of a positive belief.

Take Care of Yourself

We have a physical and mental health crisis in the United States. Our current Western medical model is incomplete and inadequate to help us fully heal and evolve. There is so much pain, violence, dysfunction, abuse and addiction in our world and it seems to be getting worse. We have become disconnected from each other and from the Earth. And the current planetary energies are intensely chaotic, volatile and stressing to our nervous systems, causing instability and fear, in some cases pushing people to mental breakdown.

We are living in unprecedented times that are pivotal and critical in the history and evolution of the Earth and humanity, and we are on a trajectory for enormous evolution or devolution. My advice to the reader on how to take care of yourself in this time is: Seek out healers of light who will help heal the whole self and help you to rediscover your connection to your own divinity and to Source/ God, someone who can help you release whatever no longer serves you on your path to healing and wholeness.

Love yourself. Respect everything on the planet and understand the sacredness and interconnectedness of life. Know that whatever one person does affects the whole. Stay out of fear. Keep your mind free from negative thoughts and images. Do not watch the news for it is full of information that engenders fear. Do not watch violent films or read material that is disturbing to your energetic field. Be in nature as much as possible to help re-set your body.

Take time each day to be in silence. How can you hear Spirit if you are not quiet? Fill your mind with happy memories and joyful thoughts. Stay away from gossip and negative talk, including negative self-talk. Be kind to everyone. Speak words that are positive and uplifting. Eat healthy food and drink clean water. Practice breathing deeply from the belly. Take care of the Earth.

The Gift

Bridging Heaven and Earth Meditation:

Imagine there is a beam of light coming down from the heavens and going into the crown of your head. This beam of light can be any color. Allow this light to move down your body, penetrating every bone, muscle, tendon, ligament, organ and cell until it comes down to both your feet. Then see the light shooting out the soles of your feet, descending down into the Earth until it reaches the very center of the Earth. Allow the energy from those beams of light to branch out and expand like tree roots, anchoring into the great Earth Mother. Just as tree roots take in the energy from the soil to nourish the tree, allow the energy of the Earth Mother to trace back upward through these beams of light, back up into your feet, moving up through your body, mixing with the energy from the heavenly light descending. Allow the new energy to move all the way up your body infusing every bone, muscle, tendon, ligament, organ and cell of your body. Now you have a joining of heavenly and Earth energies and you are the center, perfectly balanced in between the heavens and Earth, connecting the two energies and allowing them to nourish your body. You should feel both energized and peaceful, calm, centered and grounded from this exercise. Let your love and light expand out into the world. As you heal yourself, you help heal the planet. God Bless.

Chapter 8

CHAPTER 9

Beáta Alföldi is a leader in the field of shamanism, healing, personal development, spirituality, women's empowerment and leadership. She is a noted shamanic practitioner and healer, workshop facilitator, ceremonial leader and speaker. Beáta comes from an international career in professional dance, choreography, theatre and television. However, after a series of life-shattering events, she was called onto a path of personal transformation and service of the deepest kind.

Beáta completed formal training in shamanism and energetic healing in Australia and then had the privilege of travelling and living extensively in many different parts of the world, studying with indigenous elders and teachers from various spiritual and shamanic traditions.

Beáta has facilitated workshops, held opening ceremonies and given presentations and talks at the Eclipse Festival 2012, Subsonic Music Festival, Rainbow Serpent Festival and Byron Spirit Festival. She has a successful healing center in Sydney, Australia and facilitates private sessions, mentorship programs, workshops, presentations and retreats worldwide. A member of the International Energetic Healing Association, she is passionate about inspiring individuals to find the courage to live a life that is authentic, empowered, free and radiantly alive!

For more information on Beáta's work visit: www.beataalfoldi.com

Embracing Life Through Death: The Ultimate Transformation

Part of the process of working with the energy of transformation in our lives is accepting full responsibility for what we create on a moment-to-moment basis. If we truly want to transform our lives, we have to look within and transform ourselves first—a journey that is light years away from the popular notion of transformation that we often read about in most spiritual and New Age material today.

In my experience, transformation is never a glorified "bells and whistles" affair where you experience instant enlightenment and then your life changes forever. It is real, raw, and painful—wild in its sweeping away of your foundations, beliefs and perceptions of reality—a slow process that takes years of self-reflection and deep inner work to move through.

Only when we have the courage to move away from the "story" of any particular situation that we've experienced in our lives by understanding and reframing the actual trauma of the event, can we come to see the perfection and beauty of "all that is" and rename the story for ourselves. Only then can we see the larger picture in relationship to our lives, our own healing, our potential, and what these traumatic experiences might be calling us to awaken into.

Facing Devastation

I've always looked to life itself as my greatest teacher. And in 2011, life took me on the most deeply transformative and challenging journey to date, the death of my son, Alakai, who died in the process of childbirth. He was full-term.

I remember being in the hospital ward after the surgeons had given me an episiotomy before wrenching my son out with forceps. I was exhausted, shocked, in terrible emotional pain, holding Alakai's lifeless body in my arms. Grief-stricken beyond words, I recall thinking, "This doesn't happen to me. I'm a good person."

Now, I am embarrassed to admit that this was my first thought. I look back and realize my level of naivety and perhaps arrogance, which is so typical of our Western culture. Stillbirth happens to six Australian women every day. Seemingly unthinkable events happen to good people all the time.

Cradling his body, I realized the utter preciousness of life—the awareness that life can be given and taken from us at any given moment. A deep sense of humility came over me and with that humility a commitment to my son—a commitment that his death would not be in vain—that I would use the experience of his loss to somehow make a difference in the world in whatever way that I could.

Two weeks after his death, I found out that my mother was terminally ill with cancer. Not long afterwards, my husband and I divorced due to the incredible strain on our relationship. In the midst of all this pain and loss, I had absolutely no reference point to hold onto and this was nothing short of terrifying for me. But I knew I was facing a choice—to either drown in self-pity and sorrow or to go deep within and commit to a path of personal healing, transformation, and growth.

After all my years of spiritual practice, would I be able to face the greatest challenge of my life and somehow find the courage to continue to open my heart and trust in Spirit within my darkest of nights? I didn't know. All I knew was that if I didn't use this experience to create change and somehow step into the work that I was meant to be doing, I would regret it for the rest of my life.

Training

I've always been drawn to the interior spaces—to the soul, to Spirit, Earth, nature and life's mysteries. The connection that I feel with my cultural ancestry, including rituals that have deep meaning and healing power, is in my Finno-Ugric bloodline and heritage.

I was born in Hungary and at six months of age my parents escaped to Italy where we stayed in a refugee hostel. In 1971 we emigrated to Australia to start a new life. I was a deeply sensitive child and could see and feel the world of Spirit all around me, which, most of the time, was incredibly frightening for me. I remember at the age of four when I first encountered a vision of the most terrifying kind: a set of red glowing eyes underneath my brother's bed! And the visitations from other beings from other worlds didn't stop there. I was tickled under my armpits in the middle of the night by energies that I couldn't see but could only feel—energies that felt like witches with long horrible fingers and nails—menacing and terrifying to a little girl. I could sense entities in the hallway of my home, see dark figures looking over me, and hear various voices and commands. One night I was so terrified I crawled into my brother's bed for comfort.

Looking to the doorway, I felt the deepest, most uncomfortable presence. A voice in a low, menacing tone said, "Come here!" Needless to say, I didn't budge from my place of safety.

That was the last time I had such a frightening experience. Going to a Catholic school, I was familiar with the "Hail Mary" prayer and used it for protection, commanding these spirits to leave me alone. I think I finally made an unconscious pact with my higher self to never be able to see, hear or feel the presence of the spirit realms again.

It has only been in the past 10 years that I have felt safe enough to open myself back up to the subtleties and the dimensions of the spiritual and psychic world and to trust deeply in what is being shown to me. Having been through the terrible and wonderful events of my life, I know that I am strong enough and grounded enough to be able to access, understand and utilize the information in a way that doesn't terrify me anymore. Now I use these gifts to facilitate my clients.

Growing up, the only time I truly felt I belonged and was totally connected to life, to my body and to myself, was when I was dancing. After many years of rigorous training in classical ballet and contemporary dance, I received a scholarship to study in the US. At the age of twenty-one, I moved to England and spent ten years working as a professional dancer, travelling the world with my craft. This connection to the wisdom of my body and the insights I received from the felt-sense experiences in my body, still serve to inform and keep me grounded today. However, in my 20's I developed chronic sciatica—a painful condition that lead me away from dance onto my healing path through alternative medicine, shamanism, yoga and Earth-centered practices.

After becoming a certified, practicing yoga teacher, I travelled the world formally studying and training in the areas of shamanism, eco-psychology, mind-body counseling, energetic healing, ceremonial work and plant medicines. In 2007 I travelled to Peru to work with some highly-esteemed indigenous and traditional medicine men and women such as Don Augustín Rivas Vásquez, Don Rubén Orellana, Rossana Nascimento, and Javier Regueiro.

My personal study with these individuals was primarily focused on working with the plant medicines of Huachuma and Ayahuasca. I was also able to experience their unique ways of utilizing healing techniques in working with different ailments, from physical trauma, addictions and illness to emotional and psychological issues. These techniques involved soul-retrieval work, energetic extractions and deep healing involving the use of icaros (medicine songs) to move and direct energy to the group or individual.

Traditionally, these songs can be performed by whistling, singing with the voice, or playing an instrument such as the flute, drum, rattle or chakapa, a constructed bundle of leaves used to help evoke the healing effects of working with plant spirit medicine allies—conscious intelligences residing in Ayahuasca, Huachuma and all the other master plants used ceremonially for healing, connection and divination, connecting us with forces that exist beyond our immediate reality yet which have a direct impact on everyday life and well-being.

In 2008 I completed a two-year program in

Shamanic and Energetic Healing at The Awareness Institute in Sydney, Australia under the tutelage of master healers and transpersonal psychologists, Paul Perfrement and Suzanne Lewarne, learning soul-retrieval, energetic-extractions, the shamanic drum journey, core-shamanic and energetic healing techniques and principles, totem animal work, crystal therapy, medicine wheel work, ancestral lineage healing and clearing, mind-body counseling and much more.

At that point in my life I thought I was well and truly on my path as a healer. I thought I understood the transformative process. And then, in 2011, Alakai was taken from me, my world fell apart, and my real work began.

Walking the Talk

When faced with times of deep pain, crisis and hardship, our own daily spiritual practice, surrender and trust in the process of life need be embraced in order to heal. I was only free from my suffering after I had gone to the depths of the abyss, returning with the gifts that the suffering was intended to awaken in the first place.

In those moments of life's deep initiations, we are given the opportunity to truly become free—free to embrace a greater version of our becoming— taking responsibility for our lives, understanding that we are all co-creators of our reality. So often I say to people, "Who is the only person present in every situation of your life?" It's us. Me and you. In becoming more aware of that, we can begin to create in a more conscious manner. And when we realize how deeply we are connected to each other, to nature and to the totality of life, everyday living becomes a sacred prayer, a ceremonial dance in learning to create consciously.

Walking this path has transformed the very nature of my innermost being. I went from someone who didn't know what she wanted to do with the rest of her life to someone who knew exactly what she wanted. I became very clear as to how I wanted to feel, who I wanted to associate with and what I was prepared to accept and not accept in my life. I didn't realize it at the time, but everything had to be stripped away in order for me to be able to live my highest creative expression and potential. Nothing less than the total restructuring of every aspect of my former self would do.

It is because of what I have experienced, claimed, and healed through my own personal journey that I can be a catalyst of deep transformation in the lives of the people that are drawn to work with me. You cannot facilitate what you have not journeyed through yourself, and I hold up a mirror for others—a brutally honest, yet compassionate mirror. People usually come to me when they have hit rock bottom. By the time they hear about my work, they have tried many different types of approaches to their healing, usually traditional work, and have exhausted all possibilities. But if they are willing to do what it takes, once they are able to transform and empower their lives, the doorway towards experiencing their own magnificence and beauty is awakened.

Many people feel helpless with the seemingly terrible state of the world and don't know where to begin. What I always suggest is that we need to "Begin within!" That means getting into the very core of what makes each of us the way we are and asking ourselves to take responsibility for "cleaning up our own backyards" first! We cannot effect positive change until we begin the arduous journey of changing ourselves first. This includes all the stories and situations that keep us from shining our brightest light in the world.

One particular woman I have been working with over the past year came from a rigid corporate background in IT. She was brilliant in her work and received much recognition, but remained unfulfilled and had trauma from her childhood that was affecting the way she was living her life. She was shy, afraid of her radiance, afraid to be truly seen or to share issues that were important to her. Underneath these insecurities was a woman who was powerful, wanting to create real change in the world, change that would help others to also live their dreams.

In the space of just over a year, we worked together with in-depth counselling processes and core-shamanic practices such as soul retrieval, drum journeys, womb wisdom practices, breathwork activations, ceremonies, ancestral lineage clearing, totem animal work and energetic extractions; soul-retrieval, energetic-extractions, the shamanic drum journey, core-shamanic and energetic healing techniques and principles, totem animal work, crystal therapy, medicine wheel work, ancestral lineage healing and clearing, mind-body counselling and so much more.

Immediately afterward, she quit her IT job, (which she had been doing all of her life) and has now started a charity project in Cambodia which helps underprivileged children have access to computers and education.

The change in these children's lives is truly remarkable and the change in her has been even more remarkable to witness! She went from being an insecure woman who didn't understand or acknowledge her own power, to a woman who is becoming a fierce voice for empowerment through education in children's lives. It all began with her courage to change her personal story by confronting her fears and releasing her negative self-talk, thereby becoming an empowered and radiant woman with a clear vision on how she wanted to live and experience her life.

Another one of my clients, a once happy and fulfilled individual, came to me a frightened, depressed and agoraphobic woman. During a Shamanic Breath Work Activation she started to display behaviors of being possessed. She could not look me in the eyes, and the entity that was residing in her womb space started to reveal itself through contortions in her face and body. It also drove her to try and hurt both her and me through scratching and growling. I later found out the entity had been trying to entice this woman into harming herself over the previous couple of months. She had never had those thoughts before.

What we both realized was that while having an intimate sexual relationship with a man who was abusing drugs and alcohol, she had inadvertently picked up a negative energetic imprint from him which was now residing in her womb. (I see this happen often to people when they allow others into their intimate space who abuse substances, who are controlling, manipulative, violent, and disrespectful.)

Through the use of my voice, my rattle, strong

intentions and certain shamanic tools such as energetic extraction work, plus the support of my spiritual helpers and guides to assist me, I managed to remove this entity attachment. It did, however, stalk me in the dream space that evening. But I was prepared. I work a lot with lucid dreaming and was able to recognize this energetic attachment (which was obviously upset with me for removing it from its host) and was able to outwit it and send it on its way.

Speaking of dreams, I work in dreams the same way I work in my waking life, accessing different streams of consciousness. The dream world is just as real as our current lived reality. In fact, we all work, play, and travel in our dreams—most of us just don't realize it. In all the work I facilitate with my clients, I use shamanic rattles, the hand drum and my voice to channel Light Language, which are dynamic information frequencies that are planetary and multidimensional in nature. It is a powerful healing modality that uses certain sounds and tones to activate, cleanse and heal an individual, a group, or a body of land.

I also work with a team of spiritual guides which I became acutely aware of when I started to work with clients more deeply. Different frequencies started coming through me that would support me in the use of certain healing methods, such as channeling, bringing through sound vibrations to heal and activate, receiving information about accessing energetic imprints, removing negative attachments and transforming archaic structures within a person's energetic field—all processes which were beyond my understanding of how to accomplish at the time.

In every healing situation, it is essential for people to come into a state where they can access their own internal wisdom, healing and guidance—to connect and speak directly to the unconscious aspects of themselves and therefore change their internal narrative and bring all aspects of self to the table (so to speak). This happens through a process of energetic negotiation where a person reconciles their spirit and the nature of who they are as I assist them to recalibrate lost aspects of their soul parts in order to become whole again. The journey is deep and profound and completely unfathomable—an intimate and deeply humbling process of healing that stems from the deep desire within an individual to become whole again.

One client I worked with was a former detective, suffering PTSD after witnessing one too many murders and other horrors. She came to me as a nervous woman who was unsure of herself and her path forward in life. She was still suffering the after-effects of many years of service in the police force and lack of care amongst her work colleagues. After a year of consistently working together, she is now using her natural gifts as a musician to heal and inspire people through meditation soundscapes—a powerful tool that helps humans relate to their surroundings in a holistic way. Her life has completely transformed in every way. She is now studying music full-time, fostering deep friendships with others and creating the life of her dreams.

Another man I was seeing on a professional basis had hit rock bottom, was seriously abusing drugs, and had recently gone through a bitter divorce. He had no job, little hope, and no idea of what he wanted to do with his life. After working with him intensely for six grueling months, exploring in-depth, core-shamanic practices and plant medicine ceremonies with indigenous elders, he slowly healed his past and took responsibility for his life. He is now engaged to be married, is drug and alcohol free, and creating a sports center for children.

These are just a few stories of the many clients I have and continue to work with, who had the courage to take full responsibility for their lives, walk the fire of grief, trauma and loss, have the courage to do their inner-work, heal the past, and change their perspective on what happened to them. What a privilege to witness individuals turning their lives around and assisting others in their own healing process! What a privilege to see people's personal mantra change from "I am a survivor," to "I am thriving and living the life of my dreams."

The Gift

A global revolution of awakening is happening. Everywhere, I see people who are taking responsibility for their lives who are sick of the current status quo of everyone blaming everyone else for their problems and the current problems of the world, feeling helpless about how they can go about creating change. People are realizing the power of coming together with likeminded individuals to create positive, long-lasting and effective change—change for the betterment and liberation of all people, the animal kingdom, and the environment. People are realizing the power they have within themselves and the importance of resurrecting the indigenous traditions that have so much to teach us about how to live respectfully and in harmony with the world that surrounds us.

Through the study and practice of shamanic ceremonies and Earth-centered practices, individuals the world over can learn to live in harmony with themselves, Mother Earth, the animal kingdom and each other. And as we become more mindful of how to live in healthy balance within ourselves, we see greater balance and peace in the world around us.

Losing Alakai, my son, the one person that I never thought I would lose, made me absolutely fearless. Having lost everything, I had nothing left to fear other than not living up to the promises that I had made to him—the sacred contract that continues to inform my life in every way. And so it is in the world today. We have nothing left to lose and everything to gain by invoking the sacred contract we all carry within us to honor life—in ourselves, in others, and in this beautiful world we all call home.

Gratitude Prayer

Today I give thanks for all the beauty received, for all the teachings, for all the light, and all the love that surrounds me in each and every moment.

I ask the Source of all Creation to illuminate my decisions so that I can be clear in life so that I can make the choices that will fill my life with love, peace, abundance, and joy.

May I learn to live as the radiant expression of my highest creative potential and deepest embodiment of truth.

May this expression of my truest and most intimate being illuminate everything around me so that the right words pass through my lips and the right actions manifest through my life.

May I never stop being enchanted by the beauty of life within me, around me, and in all beings. May I recognize the Divine within each person, each sentient being and in nature, so that I can understand and live from the embodied experience of knowing that Spirit lives in all.

I give thanks for my life, including everything that I have ever journeyed through, for it has made me who I am today.

I give thanks for the courage and trust to follow the whisperings of the creative expression of love to continuously guide me on my journey.

And finally, I give thanks to the Earth, to the Sky, to Mother Nature, to all my Relations, and to the Spirit that moves in ALL things, now and always.

CHAPTER 10

Elizabeth Walsh has been leading transformational processes for over 25 years. Combining many methodologies in consciousness education, her work is deeply ingrained in harmonizing the masculine and feminine energies. Her work focuses on integrating mind, heart, body and spirit. Her shamanic training as a Soul Medicine Guide has spanned for as long as she can remember, but culminated intensely over the past 10 years, training directly with a Peruvian shaman. Her initiations have trained her to walk others through the levels of pain, trauma and liberation that she has walked through herself. She brings compassion, love and the embodiment of the divine feminine and mother archetype for the healing of people and our planet. She directly connects with Pachamamma, calling on the Earth's wisdom and intelligence to create harmony and unity in community. Utilizing her business, operations and marketing experience, she supports individuals in discovering their life purpose by creating maps and pathways to creatively actualize their goals and dreams. Her mission is to bring the world back to its heart, guiding people back into the innocence of their original heart. Elizabeth travels internationally and works with people from all walks of life.

She can be reached at www.thesacred.earth

Shamanism and the Resurrection of Radical Love

Culturally, indigenous people don't go seeking God. For them, God is everywhere. Life is a prayer, prayer is harmony, and harmony occurs when we see and experience everything as unique and connected. In earlier times, sacred ceremony or ritual was very much a part of daily life, a moment-to-moment honoring of food, birth, death, the hunt, the creation of tools, the seasons—a moment-to-moment recognition of our connectedness to the bigger picture of life.

Shamanism has typically been described as the ability to bridge the worlds between body and spirit. A shaman has one foot in each world, both earth and spirit. This ability to see or know what is normally unseen aids the people who come to the shaman to heal or experience a new reality for themselves. Depending on what's needed, a shaman will help people heal physically, spiritually, mentally and emotionally—a healing that often involves the use of certain powerful medicinal plants such as Ayahuasca and Huachuma.

In the indigenous world, plant teachers were, and are, the real guides revealing new constructs of reality, other dimensions, other beings and other ways of seeing the matrix we are living in. With the help of plant medicines, we can literally see the energetic lines that connect everyone and everything, exposing the painful lie that modern man has been indoctrinated into for so long: *We are separate.*

The first time I saw the lie and its matrix, I was in a yurt on a mountain with coyotes howling in the background. Shortly after ingesting the sacrament, the entire room started to change and suddenly I saw grids of colored lines that connected everyone and everything. I saw there is no separation and that everything and everyone are interconnected. Imagine a drop of water or a wave suddenly realizing it's the entire ocean. That's what it was like. When I experienced this state of oneness, it was an embodiment of divine ecstasy that altered my understanding of reality.

Unfortunately, our Western culture does not embrace the gifts life presents. Nor does it nurture exploration and a seeking of answers and experiences outside the norm. In the West, we depend on reading books to give us knowledge. And yet, in the ancient communities, sacred plant ceremonies revealed true wisdom because what was learned was experienced from source—from life itself. It wasn't something someone gave you. It *is* you. Books, the wisdom of the West, offer information. Plants and sacred ceremonies offer an experience. And it is only through experience that true wisdom can live.

Fortunately, many people today are choosing a path of re-learning, a path of remembering who we really are, rediscovering the wisdom that lives within us. And a good portion of the path to that re-learning is the resurrection of shamanism and the use of plant medicine to reawaken us to the greater reality we are a part of.

As the old power constructs are changing, the modern-day shaman teaches people how to access the sacred realms and facilitate their own healing. Ceremony has evolved into an exploration of one's individual and collective consciousness. Women and men gather in community, or in a group, to foster connection, creativity, expression, understanding, feeling, seeing, and most importantly, being. When we work with teacher plants like Ayahuasca and Huachuma, we activate parts of ourselves that we don't necessarily have access to in our day-to-day reality anymore. We connect to the source of life in a variety of ways, only understanding fully by going through the experience.

Plant medicine—sacraments—are not used to escape ourselves. We take sacraments to become more present with ourselves and our process of individual and collective growth. We take sacraments to see ourselves reflected through others, becoming the observer of self from a different point of view. Ceremony is an honor, a blessing and a prayer. It is a place to remember the Sacred and our reverence for all of life.

The Long Search

I was a somewhat sheltered girl who grew up in Westchester County, New York and Naples, Florida. When I was in high school, I remember being in a health class watching videos about drugs. It all looked so horrific. I truly believed if I ever did *drugs*, I would die. That's what I was programed to believe. Nobody ever spoke of "sacred plants" or "sacred substances" that have incredible healing properties—plants which are as far removed from the horrific substances I saw displayed in those videos as you can imagine. So I stayed far away from anyone associated with drugs. As it turned out, what society said would kill me is what birthed me.

College was wonderful for so many things, but

it wasn't the place where I could find my calling. Shamanism wasn't listed as a college major (not that I even knew about it in those days), so I spent years seeking an elusive "something" I had no reference point for. Actually, I always thought something was wrong with me because all my friends knew exactly what they wanted to do early on. My high school sweetheart became the doctor he always dreamed of being, my college roommate became a teacher. But me? After college, I used my psychology and communications studies in a variety of fields like publishing, advertising, and the film industry.

By age 37 I was working as the chief of operations of a health and healing center in Los Angeles, feeling more on my path than I ever had before. Finally, I had found work that was in alignment with my deepest values, working with energy healers, doctors, acupuncturists, and other practitioners who taught me, and others, about healthy living.

Then, in April 2007, my date with destiny arrived. I found myself interviewing a wonderful healer who said he was headed to a "ceremony." The connection I felt with him was so profound it took me off guard. Without knowing what it was, I invited myself along, thinking it was a "spiritual ceremony." Which, of course, it was. Had I fully understood what I was going to, I would have stayed in my fear bubble and not made it to my date to discover my life's purpose. But the spirit of the master-teacher plant, Ayahuasca, made sure I showed up. And once I experienced Ayahuasca, life would never be the same. Even as I write this, it's hard to believe what I experienced during that first ceremony. But here's what happened...

I was sitting cross-legged on the floor with my

eyes closed and my hands open on my knees. I felt smoke enter the tips of my fingers and travel up my right arm and suddenly my arm was moving of its own accord, in rapid, dance-like movements. I was not controlling this movement. I was being moved. I realized *This is Shakti!*—the divine feminine cosmic energy that moves the universe.

The energy moved to my left arm in the same way. Soon I felt like a 12-armed deity, levitating and dancing in the air. Even though my mind could not understand what was happening, I was in a profoundly ecstatic state of being. In fact, when I would go into the mind, trying to puzzle it out, I couldn't stay in the experience. This went on for hours. The body and spirit elements were so strong my mind finally surrendered to what was happening. It felt incredible! There was no reason to stop it—not that I could.

To this day, I believe that a divine feminine energy entered my being and activated this energetic dynamic inside me that is still with me today. Eleven years later, it is a powerful energy integrated in the core of my very being.

A New Reality

Step by step, over the course of the next several months, I was led to my teacher, a Peruvian shaman whom I've been working with ever since.

"Tell me all the secrets," I asked.

"They are all right in front of you," he replied.

Little did I know it would take ten years before I finally understood that there actually are no secrets! Why? Because the "secrets" of life are alive and available inside each one of us. The nature of reality is truly closer than our own noses. It just takes the desire and the work to see it.

During my first trip to Peru, I was sleeping on the top floor of a hut that looked out into the jungle. In the middle of the night, I was awakened to see my teacher outside my screen window. Squinting with one eye open, I was trying to figure out what he was doing there, then realized he couldn't possibly be standing there because there was no balcony outside the window. It was his spirit body suspended in the air!

He turned and disappeared. Then a vision of two other shamans I had never seen before, came forward. They were indigenous, didn't have on many clothes, were wearing jewelry, had piercings and some tattoos. I saw them clear as day as they looked straight at me. When they disappeared, an old Asian man with a long white beard came forward. When he disappeared, I was then looking in on a ceremony with people I did not know. This was not a dream. I was totally awake.

I had just been introduced to my spiritual lineage and my life's work following the ancient teachings.

Early on in my training, I realized I could see and communicate with spirits, people's ancestors and friends who had passed over to the other side. I would be sitting, working with someone, and the spirits would just appear. They would give me particular signs, like wearing the exact outfit they had worn to the person's wedding, or other specific identifying qualities or items, like hair styles, etcetera.

I also realized how easily the "normal" mind can interfere with this kind of spiritual communication. For example, one spirit came through who was the mother of the person I was sitting with. I could see her clear as day. A beautiful dialogue began and then I started seeing images of the actress Shirley MacLaine. I couldn't understand why I was seeing images of Shirley, since she was still very much alive. I was still learning to trust this new ability of seeing what is unseen, so I disregarded it in the moment. The next day at integration, I shared that for some reason during that process I saw Ms. MacLaine. The woman I had been working with said, "Oh! My mother *loved* Shirley MacLaine!"

Eventually, enough of these experiences verified to me that what I was perceiving was accurate. Gradually, I began to trust "the sight," the mode of visual clairvoyance I was developing. Eventually, it was clairsentience that really became my gift—the ability to know, see and hear through the heart— the ability to sit with an individual, couple or group, and feel what's needed in any given moment. Talk about true *connection*.

I had been seeking this my entire life! And it was a joyous homecoming. Every penny I made was invested in my shamanic education. I became a scholar of the heart—a heartist, you could say. For me it seemed that love was the most revolutionary and evolutionary force on this planet and the foundation for the New Shamanism, injecting people with the direct experience of knowing that all of life is united as one thing—"piercing the veil" in a look behind the cosmic curtain, revealing a reality we hadn't seen before, demonstrating that everything is a reflection or holograph of our own creation.

Love and the New Shamanism

Plant medicine, which is of this earth, has been utilized for thousands of years to help heal the various wounds to our innocence caused by betrayal, creating a sense of separation from life and others. Inside this fragmentation, we create a false self, or mask, that distances us from reality even further, keeping us in the trauma loop trying to "fit in" and hide the wound rather than being ourselves. Through ceremony and other acts of self-care and intimacy, we return to wholeness. Our innocence and sense of belonging are restored.

The plants open the door to remembering. You could say they are our teachers. I call them Activators. Indeed, there's a global activation taking place right now as millions of people around the world are participating in sacred plant ceremonies every week—a vital aspect of the shift into our awakening.

The New Shamanism is like a truth serum revealing that time and space are created in consciousness and that in consciousness we can go anywhere at any time; that we can heal our wounds and change our stories. The sacred plants used in this movement reveal truths and realities we haven't seen before. Which doesn't mean that these truths and realities weren't there. It's just that we didn't have access to them before.

For example, I had carried around a story of abandonment most of my life. My parents got divorced when I was young, and I felt incredibly abandoned by my father. But then, in a sacred ceremony, a video-like screen opened up before me and started literally showing me a movie about my life.

When you "journey" with plant medicine, you create a dialogue with Spirit. And in that movie Spirit showed me the contract my father and I had made on a soul level. My father gave me everything he had the first ten years of my life. Then he stepped aside so that I could find my way as a strong woman in this world, not dependent on a man. Spirit also showed me the sacrifice it was for him, even though it ended up being the greatest teaching for me. This realization changed my entire relationship with my father. My story of abandonment became a story of empowerment and I was able to relate to him in that way instead of from the old sad story. You could say I "reclaimed my innocence."

Another veil that can be pierced with plant medicine is access to past lives. Children often remember past lives because they are still very open to receiving all kinds of information. I remember in another ceremony seeing myself lying between some large rocks, alone. I had entered a past-life experience where I lived in caves. My beloved and I were healers and people that needed healing would come to us in these caves. I re-lived being killed in that cave by a woman who was very envious of me—who literally wanted my heart. It was very clear after the ceremony was complete that the reason I had been transported back to this lifetime was to help integrate a situation that was happening in my current lifetime that was similar in nature.

The beauty of ritual and plant medicine is that they show us ourselves. They empower us. They help people to understand that reality is created *through* them—that it's not happening *to* them. We learn that we are not victims of our experience. We are graced with the knowledge that we are co-creators.

The plants up-level your core frequency. This allows people to get in direct contact with how and why they are creating their reality through their beliefs, stories, emotions, and habits of mind. Some plants raise a person's vibration to a frequency of unity where they get to see the connection of all things—where they can see how the microcosm and the macrocosm are unified, getting to witness how they are creating day-to-day reality.

One of the ways this is recognized is through synchronistic events or happenings. Have you ever thought something and then a few minutes later, it actually happened? Like you thought of someone and then they called? You see the result of what you were thinking. When this happens, you get to see that you are an intimate part of how the circuit is made.

Emotional feeling delivers a corresponding image and life responds to both the feeling and the image with a complementary and spontaneous real-life reflection. For example, I'm driving my car in a busy town center looking for a parking spot. Nothing is available, but I feel I will find a spot in front of a certain shop. I drive there and *yes!* there's a parking space right there and nowhere else. Or I think of a person as I walk down the street. Ten seconds later, they walk around the corner. Or I've lost my car keys somewhere in the house. I stop and sense/feel and then my body walks to a particular part of the house and there's the missing item.

Sacred plants allow us a window to see the fundamental structure of creation, the bones of God.

In order to live in this sweet spot of existence and personal expression, recognizing our part in the dance of life, it takes a lot of self-awareness. And to get there we must be fearless of the future and find a way to embrace the unpredictability of the next moment. And the plants that we work with help us because they are designed to open the heart. Unfortunately, on the healing journey, when we go into the deep recesses of the heart, most people are faced with their pain and trauma. We don't go straight to bliss. A large part of ceremony is creating a safe environment so that people can relax into the places they need to go.

For example, this past weekend under a radiant, pink, full moon, ten people came together in ceremony in such a profoundly intimate way that we all were able to express our deepest pain. One man was healing himself from the death of his wife. She happened to be my best friend, and I was healing from her death as well, accepting the fact that I will no longer be in relationship with her in the physical realm. Another man got in touch with his deep pain of abandonment by his parents as a five-year-old child. Through his tears, he could admit that he "hated the feminine." As the group held him in that pain and truth, he felt the safety of belonging to a tribe. As a result, his feelings shifted to love and he was able to embrace the feminine in a new way inside of himself. With his shift, his wife, who was also in the ceremony, was able to soften to him because he owned his wound, rather than continuing to play it out at her expense. After he openly admitted how he felt, she felt closer to him. This also gave her permission to take responsibility for her own emotional wounds. Their relationship changed that weekend.

Another woman had been sexually abused from a very young age. This sexual abuse created a layer of protection where she cut off from her feminine expression because it wasn't safe. She went through the world in a very masculine way so she could feel powerful. In ceremony, she lay down her "sword" and melted into a feminine space that was actually safe for her. The experience shifted her on a cellular level, and for the first time in her life, she finally felt she could be in her true feminine power.

A couple who had been together for many years wanted to have a child. But they both had been so busy in their lives that there had been no time or space to energetically bring in a baby. Both had fears about going there. Throughout the course of the weekend, the woman was able to step into her full Goddess-ness. She asked her man to really show up for her and give all of himself to her. It was after this that they connected with the soul of their future son. The wife even saw him and could feel all that he is and would be. This experience completely changed the game for them in their quest to manifest this dream.

A young woman finally had the courage to connect with her father in the ceremony and ask him directly for what she wanted and needed, which was a verbally expressive love. She really wanted to create that with him. Through her vulnerability, she was able to establish a whole new connection with her father and vice versa. Another young woman in college couldn't feel beautiful because her face had broken out in acne. She was in so much pain about this. But the group was able to intimately work with her about her definition of beauty and explore how she could find an inner empowerment that would help her to feel beauty on more levels than just the physical. Through the plant medicine, she was able to soften into herself and witness the extraordinary layers of beauty within her.

All of these examples point to deep individual and collective experiences of safety, belonging and transformation created through ceremony and the judicious use of plant medicine. Coming from a place of presence, sharing and co-creating, the oneness and equality of all people are revealed. Bonding and connecting, we take a break from the mind and journey into our bodies, hearts and spirits. Listening from a different place we receive information in a new way. When that happens, we feel safe enough to come into the heart, create new meaning, and heal.

Healthy, balanced community arises from meaning-making experiences that are shared. As we learn to place more value on the circle and the collective, as the medicine of the heart becomes accepted and valued in our culture, human potential actualized through imagination and creativity will be unprecedented.

This is the radical gift of love the New Shamanism offers us all.

The Gift

If you like, you can do this practice to gentle, heart-centered music.

Heart Meditation with a partner

Face your partner

Put your right hand on their heart and your left

hand over their hand on your heart

Feel the beat of their heart and its connection to life itself.

Look into the eyes of the person across from you.

Feel the divinity of this being.

Feel the being of the being in front of you

By looking into their eyes, their hearts, their soul.

Feel this person's hopes, dreams and fears.

What is their longing?

Breathe….

Let it all just move through you and let it touch you.

See yourself in the other being

Their eyes reflecting you back to you

As you become present to your own hopes, dreams, fears and longing

Allow the experience of oneness between you and this other being.

As you allow yourself to align with this soul,

Feel your own alignment

And let anything that might be in the way,

Just melt away

Just let it melt away …

As we heal ourselves,

Those around us heal also.

The following is the Hawaiian prayer, Ho'oponopono.

One person says:
I'm sorry
Please forgive me
Thank you
I love you.

The 2nd person says:
I'm sorry
Please forgive me
Thank you
I love you.

Stay together in this energy as long as you wish. In closing, honor your partner in whatever way feels right for you.

CHAPTER 11

At age twenty, Rebecca received an undeniable calling to step away from her psychology degree and find a spiritual teacher. This led to a ten-year apprenticeship with a family of Toltec shamans and a profound awakening. Living and working with Madre Sarita and her son, best-selling author don Miguel Ruiz, Rebecca was named as Sarita's spiritual granddaughter and the one to carry on her lineage. She mastered the ancient healing traditions along with don Miguel's esoteric teachings, garnering intimate insight into the mind-body-spirit connection. Certified as an herbalist, a massage therapist, and a holistic health practitioner, she opened her private practice in 2001 and has been working as a healer and spiritual mentor ever since. She leads retreats and workshops worldwide and recently contributed to the best-selling book, *Dancing in the Unknown*. With her blend of ancient and modern wisdom and her loving, down-to-earth candor, Rebecca embodies the essence of "Shaman Sister" with the eyes of a shaman and the heart of a sister.

You can find her at rebeccahaywood.com, visit her blog, Shaman Sister Speaks, and join her social media tribe @shamansister.

Exorcizing the Ghosts of Sexual Trauma and Their Secret Shame

Memory can inhabit us like a ghost, possessing our mind with story and our body with emotion. In some cases, it is a temporary resurrection that is harmless or even beneficial. We remember, we reconcile, and we let go. We give up the ghost.

Yet certain memories sink into our bones, especially when they come with trauma. The experience of pain, vulnerability, and fear activates our biology's drive to survive and adapt. We store the cellular memory as a defense mechanism, at the ready to freeze, fight or flee. According to the study of behavioral epigenetics, emotional stress can even alter our genetic expression, passing trauma from generation to generation. The ghosts have teeth. Thankfully, science also suggests that our genetic expression is changeable through positive emotional experiences.

But there is one ghost, so ancient and so wounded that it recoils from sight—feminine shame. In the patriarchal imprinting of our cells, we hold thousands of years of violence against women. Raped, burned, owned, and cast out of the garden, Abrahamic religions alone have left a deep mark on our cells and on our souls, permeating our culture and even our spirituality. The marginalization of the feminine lies at the root of humanity's sexual shame and is the cause of its broken heart. The masculine and the feminine at war, the human and the divine separated. This was our true fall from grace, and it has left us in a state of disconnection from ourselves, each other, our nature and this Earth.

Male or female, religious or not, we share this inheritance and all of its ghosts. Our feminine souls—our very cells—cower in the knowledge that "He will kill us" while secretly agreeing "We deserve it." And our masculine cells are either castrated by guilt or abandoned to an even older anger that pounds its chest as the motherless child. The world's battle between the sexes is a reflection of this internal war within our cells—a broken polarity stuck in a feedback loop of shame, disempowerment, and trauma.

Sexual violence against women, born in an ancient lust for power, is an attack on the feminine—body, mind and soul, bearing a ghost of sexual trauma that can be intimate and difficult to exorcise. That's how it was for me. The grip of these ghosts appeared at a young age and continued to haunt me into womanhood and throughout my training as a shaman. Yet, each tear became my medicine and the call for a different kind of —revolution— an unwinding back to center, into the primordial mud of my body's hidden graveyard.

Ghost of a Girl

I grew up in the revolutionary air of New England, just inland from the 'witch' massacres of Salem, Massachusetts. I was a tomboy with three brothers, raised on the battlefield of a divorce that asked me to choose a side. My mother, a reluctant debutante-turned-feminist, swelled with pride when I told her I never wanted to marry. I relished my tomboy nature, and I fought my father and every Laura Ashley dress he bought me. Once I discovered it to be the perfect rebellion, a warrior was born.

And it was the warrior I would need to be. Before I had even come of age, my feminine being was under attack. A stranger's hand between my legs, a stalker's eyes in my room, an old man masturbating in the mall while I froze, bewildered and afraid. These incidents made me feel completely powerless. The ghost of sexual shame was stalking me on the very streets where I lived and it changed me. Suddenly I was prey and it was my feminine embodiment that brought on the hunt. I burrowed deeper into my tomboy camouflage, holding my breath.

Summers were spent at my grandfather's fishing camp in Maine—a place frozen in time with no electricity and an outhouse plastered in faded comic strips. Nights were spent playing charades by lamplight and days were an endless adventure in the woods, on the lake, or off to sea. Nature became my secret church where I whispered to the trees and swam naked in the moonlight. Maine was the sacred ground of my childhood, the last sanctum of innocence.

But at age 15 all that changed.

He's going to kill me. The words surged through my body as I lay crumpled on the floor in defeat. I had just been raped by my friend—a boy who had stolen my trust so completely that I called him a brother. It was a hazy nightmare from which I could not stir myself to wake.

I was too drunk to defend myself, pushing him away only to pass out again. Each time I came to, my body was more naked and violated than before. I watched from a distant place—his breath, his hands, his weight—as he tore into my virginity. Afterwards he flung my body across the room like a discarded doll. I didn't even feel myself hit the floor.

The violation didn't stop with the rape. I braved the intrusive hospital exam and faced the callous detective who promptly lost all the evidence. Small town rumors flew. My grandmother suggested marriage while others questioned my virtue. Before I knew it, I was wearing my rape like a scarlet letter.

That night seemed to never end. I became my own punisher, traumatizing myself with every mental replay. Fear flitted around in my body like a bird without sky. The temple of my being had been desecrated, the sacred ground of Maine tarnished, the cherished bond of brotherhood broken. Even I was not to be trusted. Feminine shame, hiding in my soul and in my very cells, rose to the surface telling me, "I deserved it"—a secret shame that ate away at me, body and soul. I tried to erase myself from this world, starving my body, my ghosts burrowing deeper. And yet, there was revolution in my blood. Soon, I would find out how much.

The Calling

The summer of my sophomore year at the University of Vermont, I took a job as a caretaker on Mt. Mansfield, the highest peak of Vermont's Green Mountain range, living solo at Taft Lodge, tucked into the mountainside.

One of my duties was called "Sunset Check" where I would ascend the peak to ensure that all its visitors had gone for the night, leaving the entire summit to myself. Each night I sat in silent meditation until the sun's last glow slipped beyond the horizon. And then one evening, as I made my way up the last rocky crags of the precipice, I heard a voice that seemed to come from within me and all around me:

You must do this now.

Although the words could have been plucked from some cheap cinematic moment, their power and meaning were instantly clear—I was to abandon my current life for a spiritual one. It was not an invitation, it was a demand. The message dropped into me with such a force that my mind was struck silent and my body collapsed onto the warm rock. I felt myself free-falling, spinning through a blinding darkness that overwhelmed my senses and splayed my heart open. I lay in that space of silence and light, its whispers rippling through me.

Find her — find your teacher.

As the last rays of the fading sun danced across my body, the first steps of my quest were revealed. I would not return to school in the fall. Instead, I was directed to quit my job the next day and head back to Maine, the scene of the crime, to collect a piece of myself I had left behind. Since the rape, I had defiantly reclaimed my beloved Maine as sacred ground. But I was a stranger in my own skin—disconnected, disenfranchised—my body still lying on that tear-soaked floor, awaiting my return.

I spent the month of August at my grandfather's camp, alone and in silence. Soon, my teacher arrived through my dreams. Every night, there she was—an old woman wielding a mirror in which my eyes became hers in a brilliant explosion of light. The dream always startled me awake, filled with a hungry curiosity. *Was this my teacher?*

There was barely time to wonder. That fall, my aunt announced a cross-country road trip to

California and I was to be her co-pilot. We were about half-way across the country, beyond the point of no return, when I finally discovered what awaited us in San Diego—a Toltec shaman named Madre Sarita.

Madre Sarita

I recognized her eyes immediately. I seemed to evaporate into them and into the unusual smell of flowers that filled the air. Her body didn't seem big enough to produce the amount of light radiating from her presence.

"Where have you been mija?" Her son translated as she chastised me with a loving slap on my knee. "I have been waiting for you! You have much to learn and we don't have much time. Nina Blanca (Death) will come back for me very soon." Such mysteries were as real to Sarita as her own skin.

Sara Vasquez, affectionately called Madre Sarita, was an 87-year-old Mexican curandera (healer). Born into a family of Toltec Naguals (shamans), she blended her ancestral ways with the Faith Healing she learned later in life, becoming renowned for her miracles, curing everything from blindness to paralysis, even bringing rain to drought-struck lands.

"I want you to be my student," she continued. "You already carry the balsam of healing in your hands and a heart that is open to all of humanity. But there is fear. Why are you afraid, Mija? Can't you see that God is with you?"

Emotion rushed through—her words touching an unknown fear of my power and even of God—the ancient wound of my feminine betrayed. A tear escaped my cheek and landed on her hand, still resting on my knee. "All that pain you endured was your preparation, teaching you compassion for the suffering of humanity," she said. "But you must have faith-in God and in yourself. With it, you will help so many all over the world. This is truth, but I cannot tell you anymore until you are ready. And Mija, don't cry! You are in the right place now."

Days later, a dream came to her son, Jaime, revealing that I was Sarita's spiritual granddaughter and "the one" to carry on her lineage of healing. I would live with Sarita and her family for the next three years, and work with her for another seven—all the while, healing myself as I learned to heal others.

Embracing the Shame

My first healing with Sarita was an Egg Cleansing—an energetic cleansing and reading in which an egg is rubbed on the body, absorbing the negative energy and taking an imprint. The egg is then cracked into a glass of water and read like an x-ray, displaying the physical, emotional, mental and spiritual influences. Sarita used an Egg Cleansing to diagnose a client's imbalance and to cleanse them in preparation for the deeper healing techniques of Fire-Cleansing or Psychic Surgery.

In my case, the egg revealed a sexual imbalance that was blocking me spiritually. The yolk was encased in sinewy cobwebs and topped with a layer of fog which pressed it down onto the bottom of the glass. She saw my ghosts right away—the shame that gripped the throat of my feminine being. She described it as my sadness and my curse, but then swiftly turned my wounded world on its head. My newfound grandmother, with her Guadalupe candle aglow, asked me how long it'd been since I'd had sex.

Sheepishly, I admitted to my prolonged, self-induced celibacy. "Mija!" she chastened. "This is not healthy. Sex is good for the body and for your energy. It is not a sin. It is consecrated by God. I have thirteen children. Where do you think they came from?" She laughed, holding her womb, then got serious as she examined my face and the emotion I was attempting to hide. "Your body was made for procreation and for pleasure—*your* pleasure."

Her eyes were so full of love that my armor fell away and my heart broke open to my sexual shame.

In time, this shame would be transformed into a reverent sensuality that connected and empowered my body as a tool of receptivity. Sensuality offers a huge source of organic and spiritual power. As I studied with Sarita, gradually moving from victim to survivor to healer, I could feel the fire in my womb connecting me to the Earth and to all of Life. It wasn't sexual, it was a biological experience of the divine. The wind on my skin, the smell of a rose, the taste of an impeccable meal—it all became spiritually sensual, as if God were making love to me.

And yet it was a long process. Judgment would continually interject, the shame would return, and my senses would shut down. In addition, sexual assault continued to be a pattern in my life, even years into my healing, the predators persisted and my fear dug in. Anyone with PTSD or the like knows it is visceral and absolutely reflexive. No matter how much you unplug the mind from a memory, the body has its own. And, as I painfully learned, the emotional frequency of shame that the body holds invites more trauma.

This was the "curse" that Sarita had seen in my egg. She called it "magia negra," black magic, saying I was possessed by an energy that was "not my own and not from this time." She prescribed two more Egg Cleansings followed by my favorite of all her techniques— Fire Cleansing.

The Limpia de Lumbre is a beautiful ritual that envelopes one in medicinal smoke while cleansing them with an egg, a salt crystal, and herbs. These are then burned in a ceremonial fire, releasing the energy to the ethers. When Sarita saw that one's illness was "unnatural," meaning that a "daño" (curse) had been placed upon them, the prescription of a Fire Cleansing was always given. She also used it to exorcise foreign entities that had attached themselves to one's life force, causing fatigue, illness, addiction, even influencing one's choices.

Sarita would see several "curses" in me over the years and smoke them out of hiding. Each trauma in my life was an emotional attachment that had congealed into "foreign entities"—a victim, a warrior, a nun, and the prostitute who sold them all. The Fire Cleansing cut those energetic chords, purifying the emotional channels in my body. But my "entities" held another anchor point—the stories that continually called my ghosts back.

Ghost Stories

Sarita must have heard them. She soon encouraged me to learn how to heal the mind with her son, don Miguel Ruiz. "The best healer is one who brings the two together," she said.

Miguel taught me the Toltec practices of Stalking, Recapitulation and Dreaming—meditative practices, each with a different focus. Stalking uncovers the mind's beliefs, Recapitulation recovers the energy from them, and Dreaming teaches us to use that energy in a different way. Through my work with him I eventually "stopped my world," as the Toltec say, meaning I shifted my assemblage point—the place from which I form myself and my reality, no longer identifying as this body, its emotions or the stories that it held.

In the process, I finally unearthed the energy that Sarita had seen in my egg: "Not my own and not of this time." I realized the story of my sexual shame was written long before I inhabited this skin. It lived in my cells, in my mother's cells, and in the mothers that came before her. *I had shared the experiences of my mother while growing inside of her— her hopes, fears, and even her memories. Had this energy been traveling from womb to womb for generations? How far back could this wounded inheritance go?*

Filled with these questions, I entered into a temazcal ceremony (sweat lodge) intent on exhuming this old energy from its resting place. The temazcal's womb-like dome represents a return to our mother— a perfect vessel for my journey. And I carried the wisdom that would fuel my healing.

The very first tool Sarita gave me was "the spiral of life"—the mechanism for "astral travel" through which the soul visits other times and places, receiving teachings or delivering remote healing. Not surprisingly, it was the most powerful temazcal I have ever experienced. I slipped into a complete trance state and travelled through my feminine ancestry, emptying out so completely that I returned to the primordial mud from which my lineage emerged and, with ghost torn from flesh, I arose anew.

But even in this sacred space of healing, lurked the shadow of the patriarch. I was due for my menses, so before I could even enter the lodge, the male "shaman" painted the skin over my ovaries with crosses to "protect" him from my energy. But I was the one needing protection. After the ceremony, as I lay dreaming by the fire, the "shaman" snuck into my sleeping bag. I was still in such an altered state that I didn't stir to my body's defense until it was too late— the crosses on my womb now smudged by his greedy hands.

"I couldn't help myself," he whispered. "Your energy was too strong. It pulled me in."

Unfortunately, this kind of abuse by men in powerful shamanic roles is not unheard of. And, like many women, I took responsibility for the whole thing, telling myself it wasn't rape, that it was part of my healing. But truly, I felt contaminated all over again—ripped from grace and hurled back into the slime of that old shame. *Will this ghost forever haunt my flesh?*

The Final Exorcism

Sarita used to say that one must receive the *name* of an offending spirit before it can be fully released. It wasn't until shortly after her passing that my last ghost was named and the key turned in the lock of this haunting wound.

Unbelievable as it seems, I was raped yet again. But this time was different—my eyes were open. I had grown so much with Sarita and Miguel that I was able to stay awake during the experience, holding witness to it without taking the man's energy on as my own. His touch never reached me. I was present, a guardian unsurrendered, and in one astonishing moment my eyes caught his and held in recognition. I saw his ghost— a little boy stood before me—a motherless child lost to his own divine feminine, shaming her as he grieved her love.

This was the wound of the male—generation upon generation of men. My mind flashed on the memory of my temazcal and I understood: the primordial mud had been calling me deeper—forcing me to see how feminine shame goes so much further than one lifetime of experiences—further even than one lineage of women—how it's steeped in the larger story of the feminine and the masculine.

Through all the years of healing I had forgiven the men who had trespassed against me and my feminine ancestry. But I had never forgiven the masculine within me—the part of myself that perpetuated feminine shame. I had finally heard the name of my lingering ghost: *the abandoned masculine,* and one more Fire Cleansing would send him home.

I entered into a semi-trance state and began the motions of the cleansing. I felt a gentle spiral begin to form, pulling me into my body and into the most complete act of forgiveness. I became the Mother, cradling the world inside of me. Every act of love and hate, I held as my own children. Waves of ecstasy and agony surged under my skin until their duality merged and, as I made a final sweep of the smoke, the primordial energy of division released. It shuddered through my body like a gentle earthquake, as if the polarity of my cells were shifting. The frequency of trauma lifted from my body, along with its secret shame.

The organic conduit of my feminine vessel had been restored. Stillness and power, only before attained in spiritual flight from my flesh, were now grounded in the fullness of my embodiment. The woman had been healed into the shaman.

Passing on the Healing

Countless women and men have come to me exasperated by the pattern of trauma in their lives, feeling disconnected, disempowered—like they can't quite shake the weight of their ghosts. But they can be healed, and it doesn't require a mysterious spiral or an "exorcism." The medicine lies within one's emotional presence.

Today's world tends to underestimate emotion as impractical, weak, unintelligent and merely reactionary—another shame to deal with. We repress, bypass, override or otherwise distort our emotions into experiences that are socially acceptable, leaving a "survivor" standing atop a "victim" who hasn't yet healed. We must embrace the pain and befriend emotion all together.

In their natural state, emotions can be reliable guides and can even self-regulate. Like the senses, emotions offer a direct and accurate perception of the external and internal world—a direct experience before the mind interprets it. When we are emotionally present, we can catch that moment and allow our organic emotions to inform us and move through us, guiding us to truth rather than into story. And when we add love to their presence, any unnecessary emotional pain or negativity naturally unwinds from the body and we return to balance.

Too good to be true? Hardly! Science reveals a truth, long known by shamans, that emotional patterns turn into thought patterns and vice versa. Both affect the body and are effects of the body's emotional history. But any emotional trauma, ancient or new, can be healed by changing the emotional input. Love the shame and the cells will recalibrate. Love your self and your cells will recalibrate—and so will those thought patterns. The brain actually remaps its neural wiring in response to emotional stimuli—decommissioning unused pathways and patterning new ones that support a language of love instead of shame.

Shamanic healing doesn't work from a script. It meets you where you are and allows your soul to lead from there. But healing and developing the emotional presence is an imperative step for clearing trauma, shame, or any psychosomatic imbalance.

My favorite way to do this is with a series of Egg Cleansings and Fire Cleansings, spread out over the course of days or even years, depending on the intent and need. This allows time for the client to deepen their readiness for each cleansing through private mentoring sessions and intensive healing retreats. I guide clients through their process using the Toltec practices I learned from Miguel, but with a feminine twist—Stalking and Recapitulating the beliefs through the emotions while Dreaming them into a healed presence in the body.

Ultimately, clients heal their relationship with the body, repossessing themselves with an emotional presence that amplifies their healing and guides their lives forward in a more connected way—embraced, embodied and empowered.

Ghosts be gone.

The Gift

Beloved
I come to you now,
Pulled by your sleeping scarlet dreams,
Your flowers of yearning,
Your earth's turning,

That I may reach into this vessel
—Beyond feast of ghost and
Pain possessing pleasure—
And bend my love into you,
Become your trestle,

'Till you rise upon my kisses
And your light breaks only into dawn
— Never a slave
To their empty grave
No more.

I have more gifts for you! Find tools and practices
at <u>rebeccahaywood.com/gifts-for-the-ghost</u>.

SECTION III
Modern Applications

CHAPTER 12

José Luis Stevens, Ph.D. is an internationally recognized lecturer, teacher, and consultant, specializing in personality and the application of indigenous wisdom to business and life. A psychologist, licensed clinical social worker, and author of twenty-one published books and self-published e-books, as well as numerous articles, he is also on the board of the Society for Shamanic Practice. He is the cofounder of the Power Path School of Shamanism and the Center for Shamanic Education and Exchange. He completed a ten-year apprenticeship with a Huichol (*maracame)* and for the last twenty-five years has studied extensively with the Shipibo of the Amazon, the Q'ero of the Andes, and continues his training with the Huichol in Mexico. His most recent books published by Sounds True are *Encounters With Power* and *Awaken the Inner Shaman.*

He has a doctorate in Integral Counseling from the California Institute of Integral Studies, an MSW from the University of California, Berkeley, and a BA in Sociology from the University of Santa Clara, California.

He lives and has his base of operations in Santa Fe with his wife and task companion, Lena. His website is: thepowerpath.com

The Interface Between Shamanism and Business Practice

I am about to ask you what you might consider a strange question: What does the path of shamanism have to offer the modern world of business, the modern businesswoman, or businessman? The reason this question may sound strange is that our Western culture has almost completely forgotten the huge, if not critical, role that shamanism has played in our survival as human beings on this planet. In fact, I would go so far as to say that the human race probably would not have survived if it had not been for the shamans who guided the earliest people, tending to their needs, teaching them how to live. Not only did they teach and lead the first humans, but they played an important role throughout history right up to the present day as leaders, teachers, and healers among the indigenous peoples of the planet.

Shamanic ways have cropped up on every continent in every region of this planet throughout all of human history despite no physical contact between shamans and cultures due to huge distances, oceans, and the lack of modern communication technology and transportation. This suggests that the shamanic ways are part of our DNA. They would arise no matter where we were, even if we established colonies on the moon or Mars.

Despite the fact that early anthropologists wrote shamans off as psychotic or strange anomalies, they have carried the primary leadership roles for their villages, tribes, and nations for thousands of years. The emperors of China and Mongolia were trained shamans with the highest of skills in martial arts, mathematics, anatomy and physiology, and the arts. They were the first masters of strategy and organization. The chief advisers to the emperors of Japan were trained shamans as were the military trainers, those who trained the Samurai in martial arts and sword-play. The Mongolians, who conquered the Chinese in the thirteenth century, were expertly trained shamans as well. The Incan, Mayan, and Aztec emperors were likewise trained shamans, as were the Druids of England. These talented women and men were no fools, no psychotics, no backwater con artists. These were the best of the best, the most competent of their people, and for a very good reason.

Training to become a shaman anywhere in the world has traditionally taken many years under the tutelage of masters of their crafts. Often the training was so arduous that a good percentage of novices and aspiring students washed out and even died in the process.

Likewise, the Native Americans, Siberians, Inuit, Tibetans, Egyptians, Vikings, Polynesians, Africans, the early Europeans, aboriginals of Australia, Southeast Asians and many more all had their shamans or equivalents. All practiced similarly as accomplished artists, able forecasters and prophets, performing ceremonies, healing their sick, leading their people in battle, acting as wise counsel, and leading their people in spiritual matters.

Ironically, in the last two thousand years organized religions have attempted to stamp shamanism out, even though all the leading religions have their roots in shamanic practices such as prayer, initiatory ceremonies, symbolic sacrifice, baptism, the use of incense, fire, singing, laying on of hands, and meditation.

But before turning to my main topic, the interface between shamanism and the business world, let me introduce myself and tell you about my earliest association with shamanism and how it came to play such a large role in my life's work.

Educational Interface

When I was a small child I spent much time with my Mexican grandmother who was my babysitter during the years when my parents both worked as lighting experts in Hollywood during the late forties and nineteen fifties. I go into much more detail about this story in my book *Encounters With Power*, a book about shamanic stories from my life. My grandmother was raised on a hacienda in Chihuahua, Mexico, in a wealthy family that owned cattle and silver mines. Like many of her generation, indigenous servants from the tribes in the area raised her and taught her their ways. They were Tarahumara, Huichol, and Yaqui Indians, all steeped in the shamanic ways of their ancestors. From them she learned healing techniques and how to look at the world from their perspective. These were the stories she regaled me with when I was a small child and, of course, I was in awe of them.

I received a Jesuit education in high school and university where I earned a degree in sociology, continuing on to the University of California at Berkeley where I received a master's degree in Clinical Social Work, then worked in hospitals and mental health centers for ten years. During this time I spent years issuing a variety of psychological tests to individuals with mental disabilities to help qualify them for government assistance.

I decided to get my doctorate in counseling psychology and specifically looked for a program that would include shamanism as part of the curriculum. I found it at the California Institute of Integral Studies, a wonderful and accredited program. There I did my dissertation on the interface between western psychology and the worldwide practice of shamanism and it was right afterward that I was to meet a Huichol maracame (teacher) who my wife Lena and I apprenticed with secretly for the next ten years.

Throughout these years I maintained a private practice and became an expert in personality styles based, in part, on my years of testing people. This naturally led me to work with a great many people, many of whom were in the business world. Many asked me for help understanding their associates, their staffs, and their customers. In addition, I worked in the legal world as a legal and jury selection consultant, participating in many egregious birth injury trials with hugely successful outcomes. Of course, much of my knowledge was gleaned from my shamanic training in combination with my psychological education. The more amazing the outcomes the more I wanted to study the shamanic ways, and I spent a good deal of time traveling to study with shamans around the world. I was particularly interested in the Paqos of the Andes and the Shipibo of the upper Amazon in Peru whom I have trained with for over twenty-five years.

So now that you know this rather strange tale of my journey through conventional education and the much stranger world of shamanism, let's turn to my theme, the intersection of shamanism and the business world.

Universal Rules of Power

One of humanity's major activities throughout history has been our engagement in business, whether through trade, lending, manufacturing, marketing, selling services, and all the things we associate with the fundamentals of business today. The activities of shamanism and the engagement of humans in business historically were not separate, but rather they were blended in the natural course of living. For example, ancient trade routes had to be defended from highwaymen and thieves and this could be partially accomplished by security forces and armies. In addition, shamans developed methods of protecting these routes in more invisible, but nevertheless highly effective, ways. Chinese Taoist shamans accompanied the ocean-going ships that mapped the world in the process of opening up trade routes for their goods. The shamans protected their ships from sinking in storms and helped to navigate invisible hazards in unknown waters. Often the shamans were the captains of their ships.

Shamans taught their people the universal rules of power necessary to becoming highly successful in the world. They taught the use of intuition, methods of understanding the symbols of nature, observation of synchronistic events to better succeed with their endeavors. They studied animal behavior to understand their methods of survival, their vitality and strength, their efficient movements, and their methods of hunting From these observations they developed the martial arts that eventually found their way to influencing approaches to business. With these understandings in mind, it is easy to see how the methods of the shamans and the fundamentals of business developed hand in glove.

You could write these activities off as mere superstition. But, if you look around at the dominance of business in the world today, you can't help but wonder what would have happened without the specialized mastery of the shamans. The most successful business peoples of the past either had shamans in attendance or were trained themselves in the shamanic arts and methods. So, what happened to divide this natural partnership such that today's world of business has completely forgotten its roots?

Most business people have no clue about the historical marriage of shamanism and business. Even if they did, they might say, "Well I'm glad those superstitious days are over. Just look at how far we've come. We have never been so successful, so dominant, so evolved."

Evolved? Well, that depends on our definition of evolved. If we mean completely dominant in the affairs of human beings, then yes, this would be accurate. If we mean controlling the lives of most people on the planet, then yes, this would be so. If we mean putting billions of people to work and raising the standard of living for millions, then yes, that is accurate. However, if we consider that business is now so divorced from its natural roots it has become a possible contributor to the destruction of the planet, then, no, not so evolved. So, you can see arguments can be made either way and both are true. Here I am advocating for the end of the divide between the shamanic ways and the current ways of business. Only when they are back together can we have a highly successful and helpful business world adopting the values of life giving shamanic practice.

When a number of highly respected astrologers and forecasters were asked what the single most important event of the last five hundred years has been in the transformation of the world, they responded to everyone's surprise and even shock, with, "The return of Shamanism." This is quite shocking when you consider several things. Most people don't even know what a shaman is anymore. For most scientists, other than some quantum physicists who know better, shamans still appear to be highly superstitious, crazy individuals who have nothing to contribute to today's world and should be allowed to quietly die out. How, then, could their rise in influence be considered in some circles to be more important than the invention of the computer or the development of the internet?

Let us consider these interesting facts: There is a little known tribe in Togo, Africa called the Dogan who live in grass huts without electricity or plumbing who know exactly the mathematics of space. They know exactly the distance from the Earth to the moon, from the Earth to the sun, the distance to the suns in the Pleiades. They know that the Pleiades are our neighbors in the same arm of this galaxy as the Earth. They consider the Earth to be a part of the Pleiades. When asked by scientists to explain how they know these things they said simply, "We know because we go there all the time. We know the people that live there."

A man I know well fell and broke his arm badly and after medical attention it simply was not healing after a number of months. The doctors did not know what they could do for him. So, he attended an Arapaho healing peyote ceremony that was dedicated specifically toward healing his arm. His friends and relatives attended. The peyote ceremonialist, or Road Man as they are called, conducted the ceremony for several hours, during which time they all consumed the usual peyote medicine. Around midnight the Road Man called him up to the fire and said, "Let's take care of that arm." He sang vigorously and then, popping a large white-hot ember from the fire directly into his mouth he held the ember and blew loudly through his teeth onto the broken arm. Right away my friend sensed that something had changed. He could move it and the pain was gone. The next day he could use it perfectly. Upon having an x-ray it was discovered that his arm was totally healed.

A Native American shaman was interviewed on the radio about his reputation for bringing rain and changing weather patterns. He was largely ridiculed on air and made into a huge joke by the interviewer. He was not pleased. Even though there was a severe drought and clear blue skies outside with no predication for rain in the future, he announced that there would be a severe storm that would create flooding in that city, that very afternoon. Of course no one believed him. That afternoon a few fluffy white clouds appeared that quickly turned into a massive thunder storm that flooded the streets of the city. His Indian name was Rolling Thunder.

I could go on and on with these stories, but hopefully you get the idea that there are trained shamans who still exist that are capable of conducting what we currently view as supernatural feats. Just imagine what could happen if they were enlisted to help and support the planet in its current state of global warming crises? The truth is, as we run out of solutions and throw up our hands in despair, that is exactly what is going to happen. We are going to ask them to help us, and once again they will take on their roles as advisors, healers, and helpers in ways that we cannot even imagine.

Once again the shamans and the quantum physicists, using different words, are going to agree on the nature of reality and how the world actually works. Out of that agreement will come miraculous solutions, and once again the world of business will benefit enormously from their presence. If this marriage does not take place, we are in such deep trouble that perhaps we will not survive our own foolishness.

Now, let us look momentarily at how shamanic methods, techniques and wisdom can interface with the world of business in profoundly beneficial ways.

The Use of the Two Attentions

Most people believe there is only one main way to look at the world, and that is through the method of rational analysis. We should be solidly intellectual and remove all emotionality and creativity from our thinking. Well, there go all the artists, all the musicians, all the dreamers, and all the mystics. However, shamans believe in two states of attention. They believe you have to have a foot in both worlds, the world of everyday appearances and the Spirit world that co-exists with the physical world but reveals different facts and information about how to do things.

The first attention I already described above. But

the second attention is more like dreaming, more like using creative imagination to solve problems, not simply analysis. In fact, what shamans would say is that if you approach life based on what you already think is true, you will never see any new truth because you are not looking for it and won't be able to see it. Quantum physicists would, of course, agree. Shamans basically say you have to get out of the box in order to really see all the possibilities. Of course, some of the most successful inventors of all time used these same approaches. People like Leonardo de Vinci, Steve Jobs, and Nikola Tesla all exhibited shamanic thinking and each contributed to the world in an outsized way.

The shamanic journey is a tried and true method for solving any number of problems. It is usually accompanied by sonic drumming that drives the neurology in our brains in such a way as to come up with amazing information in response to posed questions or concerns. It is simple, can be done almost anywhere, does not cost anything, and has helped people solve a wide variety of challenging questions, including questions related to business, legal problems, scientific questions and the like. I have used this technique to great success in my interface with the legal and business worlds.

Most people do not know this, but many of the ancient Greeks from whom we have derived so many benefits were trained practicing shamans. Recent evidence is revealing that the ancient Greeks traveled on foot to Mongolia, Tibet, and Siberia to bring back shamanic methods and ways of pursuing knowledge in non-traditional ways. Anthropologists are now learning that the Greeks used a shamanic practice called incubation, ensconcing themselves in caves and shutting out all sounds and sights, going into a kind suspended animation—a deep trance if you will—in order to speak to the ally, an ancient goddess of the times. Parmenides, considered the father of modern logic, is now known to be a shaman, an incubator, and master of speaking with the goddess. In those days these Greek incubators spoke for the goddess in symbolic poetry that is hard to decode. They listened to the goddess and brought back great wisdom and advice which they communicated in this colorful and creative poetic style. As it now turns out, the later translators of this material interpreted the words all wrong. They mistranslated material found chiseled into stone tablets and walls. And some of these mistranslations had world-changing consequences.

As it turns out, Parmenides, the trained shaman incubator, brought forth information from the goddess saying that logic could not be totally trusted to get at the truth; That intuition, the second attention, was more reliable. So the entirety of our Western culture's faith (obsession?) in logic turns out to be hinged upon a mistranslation. We went down an alternate road relying solely upon analysis, statistics, and scientific logic, when, as a shaman, Parmenides taught the exact opposite!

Now we are on the brink of destroying the resources of our planet, deeply entranced by tools that are not reliable because they are incomplete and have no heart. And this is the key to the whole topic we are talking about here: Heart. For shamans, there is nothing without the path with heart. For them, anyone or anything that is disconnected from the heart cannot possibly be in harmony with our environment and Mother Nature. Of course, humans are, by nature, creatures of heart. So use of the second attention must and will return us to heart-centered ways of doing business.

The Shamanic Rules of Power Applied to Business

Another way that shamanic perception can be extraordinarily helpful in business is to consider how shamans view and handle power, bearing in mind that shamanism is actually a system of systematically acquiring, storing, and managing personal power. Ordinarily our perception of power is quite different from the shamanic understanding of power, and this difference in perception leads us to pursue entirely different strategies to become powerful.

Unfortunately, our very externally-oriented understanding of power causes us to pursue power in many unfortunate ways that often lead to no power at all. The main difference in perception lies in opposite pursuits. We can try to become powerful by acquiring the external trappings of power such as impressive offices, vehicles, bank accounts, name dropping, photos with famous people, complex charts and statistics, even copying our competitors and so on, or we can pursue what the shamans call internal or invisible power.

Invisible power is gained by understanding the true nature of power according to basic shamanic principles. I will mention only a few of these principles applicable to doing business here because of space considerations:

1. One can only become powerful by associating with those people, places, or things that have

real power. With this understanding a person may gain infinitely more advantage in their business by spending a few hours in the sun at the beach absorbing the release of energy from the waves than from attending a get rich quick seminar. Who or what are your allies? The sun, the moon, the wind, a hawk. You will surely fail without them.

2. One must bid for power to become powerful. Anyone can bid for power at any time, but one must be ready psychologically, emotionally, physically, and spiritually or they will suffer a humiliating defeat. Timing is everything in your bid. A bid for power is a risk and does contain a cost. The cost is your investment and commitment from your heart and your comfort level. Notice there is no mention of finances here.

3. Becoming powerful depends on your trust in listening to the second attention. This is critical. Only those who trust their intuition can become truly powerful. When is the last time you acted from a hunch instead of cold data?

4. The smaller the degree of separation, the greater the power available. How much separation do you have between you and your teams, your customers, your support staff including the maintenance people, your suppliers etcetera? Are all your departments at war with each other? Or are they one big cooperative family with specialties?

Each one of these principles can be unpacked for much greater understanding. Here they have been highly summarized. Should you be interested you can read my book *The Power Path: The Shamans Way to Success in Business and Life* and discover much more.

The Gift

Here is a little shamanic exercise for you to increase your ability to use some of these principles:

Begin by finding a private space and time where you will not be interrupted for about fifteen minutes. Turn off all devices. Sit comfortably with spine erect and hands and feet uncrossed. You can close your eyes if you wish between reading the steps in the next simple instructions.

Recall the last time you made a bid for power related to your job or your business. How did it go? Consider these things: Was it worth it? Was it something that committed your heart or was it a cold, calculated move based purely on external motives? Were you ready? Was the timing right? What were the costs? How were you tested along the way? Did you pass these initiations? Who or what were your allies? Did you have any? Totem animals, inner guides, teachers, elements, aspects of nature?

If you failed, what did you learn about becoming more powerful?

Now turn your attention to your next bid for power? Does your motive come from your heart? Are you ready in all the necessary ways? Who or what are your allies? How will you be tested? There will be an initiation or perhaps a series of them. What will be the costs? Is it worth it?

Now, if possible, step into the outdoors, or at least look out the window. Let go of all your considerations and relax your shoulders. Take a deep breath. Look around. What do you see, feel, or hear out there? Is there anything that might be telling you something about this new bid and perhaps your next step? A bird flying by? A dog barking? The shape of a cloud forming in the sky? An itch on your arm? A sudden breeze? A child laughing? The position of the sun or moon? Your subjective sense of yourself?

What are the signs and symbols? Use your imagination. Be playful. If you had to choose to go ahead with it or not based on what you are seeing, sensing, feeling, or hearing, what would you do?

Do this often as a practice for various endeavors.

I hope that in this short chapter you have gained some appreciation for how shamanic methods and business practice can once again work together for great benefit. The business people I know who bring these together are phenomenal human beings. Not only are they highly successful, but they seem to be having much more fun at their work, a grand adventure. I wish you many blessings on your journey.

CHAPTER 13

David H. Milgram is a holistic chiropractor at Turtle Island Healing Center in Flagstaff and Sedona, Arizona. David is a trailblazing doctor with many healing tools in his toolbox.

His "energy-based" approach to the physical body has helped many regain their health. He applies the spinal chiropractic principle of Structure = Function to the whole body and cranium.

For forty years, he's worked with many of the greatest cranial-oriented doctors in the profession. His present interest is learning about the effects of concussion upon the human brain and how to accurately assess and treat them. Known as "The Human Whisperer," David has developed a healing system called *Positive Body Language*.

A graduate of Ricker College in Houlton, Maine with degrees in psychology and English, he graduated from Northwestern College of Chiropractic in St. Paul, Minnesota in 1982. After getting married the next day, David moved with his wife to the Southwest where they raised two sons and have lived ever since. A hiker, songwriter and musician, David is also a big student of cryptozoology, and is especially interested in stories that look, smell, and sound like Sasquatch.

For more information please contact David at: (928) 774-2272

Confessions of a Reluctant Shaman

What's happening along the journey from cradle to grave in this life is an inscrutable process. Understanding how an individual soul rolls from their last grave with their previously developed potentials, talents, and abilities, to rock back into the cradle of their next incarnation with the ability to express the essences of those very same qualities is perhaps the most magical, if not the greatest of all shamanic tricks in the whole holographic, quantum-leaping universe.

Some babies are born in a hurry and others are born slow. Some of us are born saying, "Yes!" Others are born saying, "No!" Some naturally play in a major, upbeat key vibration while others resonate with a more somber minor one. Some children are fiercely free and independent by nature, while others are just looking for someone to tell them what to do—or perhaps for a stake to burn on. Me? I grew up as a black sheep in a white family of Jewish atheists and agnostics. You see, I always wanted to know who God is.

My mother tells me that when I was three, I was sitting by one of the wheels of my grandfather's truck. As I sat next to the tire, gazing at it in an admiring way, a neighbor, who was Christian, came walking up the driveway and asked me what I was looking at.

"Looking at God," I responded.

"Oh, really? Where do you see Him?" she asked.

"In this wheel," I told her.

"Oh. Is God in that wheel?"

"Yes," I said, "God's in all wheels."

"Is that where God is?"

"Uh-huh," I told her. "God's in everything round and loves everything round. The sun, moon, earth and stars are round, and all the seasons go round."

She stood there, marveling for a 'Hallelujah' moment, and said, "Out of the mouths of babes thou hast ordained strength," before continuing into my grandmother's house where she promptly told her and my Jewish mother about the things I told her. "We may not be of the same religion," she said. "But you certainly raised that boy right."

Some people are natural born clairvoyants. They "see things" apparently distinct from the time/space continuum they're in. Others are naturally born with the particular gift of clairsentience. They "feel things" at a distance and may seem to access deep knowledge from beyond what's local. I am, by nature, a clairaudient person. I hear a voice inside speaking messages that inform me of things regarding people I'll run into soon, cool places to check out while I'm hiking, and how events in the world will develop.

In 1964, when I was seven, my Dad took me to IBM headquarters in White Plains, N.Y. on a Sunday morning to see one of the first lasers ever developed. We stood in front of this window where it was sealed off. I looked at the intensity of the light and my inner voice said, *Later, many things will be run by laser.* I wondered if that was really true. The voice kept rambling. *In your lifetime, people will fly by putting a backpack on.* "No way," I said, "like the Jetson's?"

Yes.

"What else will I see?" I asked the invisible voice.

You'll see electric power be generated by the ocean's tides.

All these things are happening now.

When I first told my mother, the psychologist, about the voice in my head, she said I was probably having an auditory hallucination, or I was in a hypnagogic state (the transitional state from wakefulness to sleep), or both. Hearing this explanation, I knew the voice was worth exploring and listening to.

From the time when I was a young child, all I dreamed of was to become a pro-baseball player. I had no idea that I'd become a professional within the healing arts as a holistic-oriented cranial chiropractor. But, like many healers, childhood experiences planted the seed of what was to come. I experienced plenty of intestinal disorders that came with a variety of doctor's names attached. My first experience of natural healing came at age 12 when my parents took me to see an M.D. in New York City who was a trailblazing allergy specialist. He told my parents to take wheat completely out of my diet for one year.

"What? No pizza?" I complained.

Back then, in 1969, there was white bread or nothing, and almost all people believed that what you ate had absolutely nothing to do with your health. My mother made cornbread for me throughout the following year, and all the ache in my belly went away. What a surprise! This opened my mind to explore the various factors that influence a person's health and healing ability, especially those that are hiding in plain sight.

The first experience where I awakened to the power of using my hands to generate healing energy occurred when I was fourteen. I took a bike trip with fifteen teenagers for two weeks riding from Montreal, Canada to Cape Cod. While going through Vermont, south of Burlington, I was awed by the natural beauty—the trees forming a canopy of shade above the road. I was a few miles behind my group when suddenly a squirrel fell from the treetops from at least a hundred feet up. As it hit the pavement my back tire clipped its tail. I scrambled off my bike and ran to the squirrel as it lay convulsing in a slowly expanding pool of blood.

Without thinking, I put my hands a few inches above the squirrel's head and prayed over and over, "Oh, God, if there is one, please help this squirrel to be all right. Please, let it heal. I'm sorry if I had anything to do with it being any more hurt. But please, let your healing energy come through my hands now and let it be done before I get any further behind my group."

There was no response.

Inside my head, I could hear the voice of my closest uncle, a sworn atheist, laughing, saying "See kid? There's no God." And I thought to leave the squirrel there and move on. But my inner voice said, *What if you simply need to repeat your prayer again for it to be answered*? So, I asked God again to flow through my hands to heal the squirrel.

It didn't work.

But I kept hearing the inner voice say, *Pray again*, even while still hearing my uncle's voice intermittently laughing, saying, "Don't waste your time. You'll get further behind your group. There is no God that hears you."

I thought maybe my uncle was right. I was a fool for believing there could be a God. Religion was all wishful thinking for the fearful and the insecure in heart and mind. But that other little voice inside me kept insisting, *What if you just need to pray one more time*?

So, I repeated my prayer again. Suddenly, lo and behold, the squirrel picks its head up out of the blood, looks me directly in the eye with total amazement, jumps up, and runs full speed into the woods. I got back on my bike and rode on down the road singing, "Hallelujah, God lives."

The second experience where I awakened to the power of using my hands to generate healing energy occurred when I was sixteen. A friend and I had gone to an Emerson, Lake, and Palmer concert in Madison Square Garden in NYC. Our seats were right next to some enormous speakers. The music was great, but when we got back to the suburbs around 3 a.m., we both had ginormous headaches and were a little hearing impaired. Neither of us could get to sleep. After a while the temple pain got so intense it zapped me like a mother of invention.

Spontaneously, I put my fingers on both sides of my temples. I noticed one side was pulsing very strongly and the other not. I intoned to myself, "When I get these pulses to balance, my headache will go away." Slowly, I began to very lightly press and pry, gently push and pull, and tap different places all over my head and upper neck. Each time I intuitively roamed around my cranium, I consciously returned to check the temples to see if anything I did helped the pulses to balance. After twenty minutes, a balanced circulatory tone and rhythm returned. My headache quickly dissipated and I got to sleep.

In the morning, my friend said he hadn't slept all night because of a bad headache. I asked him if I could try on him what I'd recently learned. To my surprise, his temple on one side also had a much greater pulse than the other. With not much more than a feather's touch, I pushed and pulled, and pressed and pried on multiple cranial and upper spine points. Each time I kept returning to his temples, as I had with myself, to see what balanced the pulses. Within twenty minutes, his headache went away.

Two for two, I thought. *Maybe if I knew what I was doing I could reliably help others*!

I had no idea I was practicing the age-old cranial science and art of Chinese pulse balancing on the greater wings of the sphenoid bone. Encouraged and intrigued, I started reading books on the natural healing arts mostly written by naturopaths and D.C.'s. I had no idea D.C. meant chiropractor until one cold winter's night a casual vision guided me through the biggest healing door of my life.

I was attending Ricker College in Houlton, Maine, about a mile from the Canadian border. One night in mid-January, a friend and I were winter camping deep in the Haynesville woods, a place legendary for Bigfoot and other cryptozoological creatures. As night fell, we sat on either side of the campfire. My friend had a slender-type build, but the fire's glow made him appear to be a very fat man. *Maybe, I thought, I'm seeing him how he used to be*? So, I asked him, "Were you ever fat?"

"No", he said. "Why do you ask me such a weird question?"

"Oh, I don't know," I said. I didn't want to weird him out by telling him I was having a vision of him. So I changed the subject and asked something safe. "What does your Dad do anyway?"

"He's a chiropractor."

"What does a chiropractor do?" I asked.

"He adjusts people's spines to help relieve back pain, headaches, and many other problems."

"You're telling me a chiropractor can actually help people feel better with his bare hands?"

"That's right."

Instantaneously, I heard my inner voice distinctly whisper: *Yes! This is your path. Follow it and you'll help many and heal a few. You'll meet everyone you need to meet for your own healing. And you know how much healing you really need.*

I twisted my arm behind my back, essentially saying, "Twist my arm, God."

The voice continued. *Just put yourself in service to all who ask for your help and treat them all the way you'd like to be treated. Always believe that you have more to learn, and remember to listen carefully to all those who'll be coming to see you later.*

The Fat Man vision became the guiding light for the rest of my path in life.

Training

One person's mysterious shamanic magic is another person's logically understood science. Magic and science may appear to masquerade for one another.

When the Native Americans first saw the white men, they thought they were all magicians because they'd point a big stick at people that would make a loud noise and even the strongest of those pointed at would fall over injured or instantly die. In truth, guns were no magical power of the white man, but rather a creation of mechanical science.

Conversely, when the early colonists witnessed Turtle Island's natives doing elaborate ceremonies with stones, bones, plants, animals and prayers to call in the thunderclouds, to induce a trance, and the rain to fall by performing a dance, and the hard rains would fall, the immigrants would say, "That's magic!" And yet the practice of rainmaking to help restore balance and harmony to the earth is an age-old science to the minds of the Native Americans.

Like the rainfall, the magical healing energy of life flows from above down and from the inside out. ADIO. Above-Down. Inside-Out. Or "to God"—a-Dio. The human being is basically an upside down tree with its roots in the sky. The rain is akin to the cerebrospinal fluid within. The cerebrospinal fluid (CSF) waters the roots of the brain tree from above, running from crown to rump, juicing it with the potential for electricity to flow via the nourishment within its liquid love. CSF also provides a waterbed for the brain and spinal cord, internally buffering them from the effects of gravity and physical shock. Cerebrospinal fluid is the real healer behind the veils.

Coming into this world after having spent some time mulling over what we'll do in this life, after being in the womb, the birthing process begins when our mother's oxytocin, also known as the "let-down" or the "love" hormone, is released. During delivery, we go from above down and from inside of our mother's body out into the world. As we grow up along life's path, the secret of generating a healthy life, filled with a downpour of healing energy and love is in letting the flow of ADIO guide us, integrating and attuning our body's alignment and mind consciousness with life.

In 1977, I graduated from Ricker College in northern Maine with degrees in psychology and English. The next year I went to Northern Arizona University in Flagstaff, Arizona to take care of my pre-requisites for chiropractic school. The following year I entered Northwestern College of Chiropractic in St. Paul, Minnesota. While in chiropractic school I began studying Sacro Occipital Technique (SOT) developed by Dr. Bertrand "The Major" DeJarnette.

I graduated chiropractic school in April of 1982, got married the next day, and moved to Gallup, New Mexico, where I apprenticed with the late great Dr. Joseph Runyon, a master craniopath with three other doctorate degrees. In 1983, after learning many tricks of the old masters to help sick people get well through nutrition in combination with soft tissue or traditional chiropractic adjustments, I moved back to Arizona to establish my holistic-oriented practice in Flagstaff and Sedona.

Early on I was asked to provide my services to Grandfather David Monongye, a Prophecy Keeper of the Hopis. I met the legendary Chief of the Rainbow Tribe in his village two days later. The "Old Turtle" was purported to be 101. After working on him, he said, "You must be a real medicine man. I can see and hear you better."

After that I was more certain than ever that I was

on my right path in life. He sent me to visit other old Native leaders and chiefs. Within three years I had three dozen patients over age 75 and several over the age of 100. Many elders were partially or completely missing the function of an arm or leg, or an eye or an ear. One man who was 112 years old had been blind for 10 years. I adjusted him and his vision returned for three years. Whenever any of these seeming miracles happened, I always gave these "Holy People," who were adept at holding the sacredness of prayer deep in their hearts despite outer circumstance, the credit. It is never just "me" doing the healing, and working with these ancient ones made me pray very deeply in order to tune in and find what to do for them and how to do it.

Perhaps the greatest guide for a healer, whether practicing shamanism or not, is to learn to get out of one's own way, having no agenda while keeping goals in mind, trusting the flow of how you're guided in the moment. Over the years there are many ways that I've come to tune into unseen information, to trust the knowledge in the patient's body and to utilize the wisdom that spirit beings—who are ever present—offer in order to help encourage health and wellness within myself and in those I'm called upon to serve.

Sometimes, I hear strong guidance to extend healing energy to a particular person who I later find really needs it. One night, a few years ago, I had a dream where a doctor friend in the Spirit World told me to go help his wife who was severely ill. When I woke up, I chalked it up to the realm of fantasy, and brushed the dream off. After breakfast, I heard the Old Doctor in my head telling me to immediately call his wife and that dream was indicative of actual reality. I called her and she said she was very dizzy and could hardly breathe. She said she felt like she was just about to croak. I went right over to her house and worked on her for about four hours. After neutralizing many gnarly negative things and assisting her to reconnect her positive energy, she was back to her normal, regular self.

Experiences like these have taught me to trust the inner voice. It's amazing all the information that a non-physical being can track and convey! Equally amazing is how my life and conscious awareness has expanded the more I let go and "fine tune" myself to Spirit's voice. There is so much more to this world and ourselves than we normally allow ourselves to know—a refinement of information is constantly available to us, and tuning in to those more refined levels changes everything.

For example, I've learned there are two basic textures of nerve sensitivity in people. Some people are energetically fine and some are coarse. Most women are energetically like silk, sensitive and smooth, whereas most men are like burlap, insensitive and rough. I don't know how else to describe it. One of the big reasons for this difference between women and men is because most women have 35 to 65 percent more fibers in their corpus callosum (the bridge between left and right hemispheres in the brain) than most men. This is essentially why women are smarter. They think with both their right intuitive and left logical sides of their brain, whereas most men think with one little part of their brain (if they're lucky), believing they're getting the whole picture!

In some way, shape, form, or dimension, we're always attending the holy rites of shamanic initiations. The chief components driving the body's cells to work, to function, are enzymes. These catalyzers create cascades of changes using barely any energy of their own. The essential magic of enzymatic function is akin to the way a shaman works to encourage positive change within themselves and those they help. Performing what look to be the smallest of acts, their little gestures of recognition and honor, enzyme-like, may serve to catalyze the flow of great waves of healing energy. Which brings me to the story of when a hummingbird flew in the front door while I worked at 7 Centers Yoga Arts in Sedona, AZ.

It flew a little tilted to one side and made a funny buzzy sound as it flew up to one of the skylights. I opened the side door and walked under the bird, saying, "C'mon. Get out of here. There's nothing in here for you."

You don't know that, my inner voice said. *Maybe he's come to the perfect place.* Just then the hummer dropped to the floor and hopped behind the stereo. So I went over to check him out.

Before you pick him up, imagine he's as delicate as a butterfly. Get really soft inside. I closed my eyes, slowed my breathing and softened myself as much as possible. Then I picked the hummingbird up, nestling it carefully in my palms. Ah! I feel and see that the range of motion of one wing is restricted and twisted.

Adjust the wing gently.

"Really?" I questioned.

You felt it. You found it. Now fix it, otherwise this bird will never fly right.

I made a tiny directional adjustment and felt a little mini-pop. Then I stepped outside the open door with the hummer in my palm. Away it flew, un-tilted, with no funny buzzy sound. The real magical shamanic part was that for the next few hours, a hummingbird-like pulse intensely vibrated through all the nerves, blood vessels, and acupressure points of my whole body. It felt like a gift of healing energy being given back to me from the hummingbird spirit for giving the little one back its wings.

The Gift

I had a friend who had a heavy machinery accident and he partially severed his spinal cord and lost the function of both his legs. I sat with him in his hospital room a few days later. While in there, he looked at the IV in his arm and asked it, "Why did this happen to me?"

As I left, I realized that my personal IV is my Inner Voice. In that moment I determined I was not going to wait until something negative happened to inspire me to listen to its messages. I encourage you to do the same.

The most important thing in life is to be on your path. Those who decide to intensely cultivate their shamanic nature and walk a healing path, usually do so because they have to—because of their own state of health and/or for assisting those they love. But you don't have to walk the path of a healer to be in touch with Spirit.

The best way to tune into the information, to attune to the knowledge and utilize the wisdom that comes from dimensions that transcend our three-dimensional world, is to use them as your inner practice. The way to gain the trust of the spirits that are guiding you is to *write down every little thing that they relate to you,* even if just on a piece of scrap paper. When the spirits see that you are really going to receive what they teach you, they want to give you more amazing graces to share in the healing services of honoring life, light, and love.

Some people are afraid of a voice within. They think it's of the "Devil" or something bad. But the way to know if a voice inside is good or bad and whether you should listen to it or not, is to source your own motivation in relation to it. Quite often, the way to know if a voice is to be trusted is to realize the underlying agenda of its message.

Remember, the body is the Earth. All of her spots are sacred. Some of her spots are very sacred—like the heart. Some of her spots are very very sacred—like the pituitary and pineal glands. You can go to the sacred spots, like the lungs, or the top of your head or temples, and receive a blessing, if you go with a good attitude and prayer.

CHAPTER 14

Joel Crandall, founder of the VOILÀ Method of Structural Joint Balancing, Kinesiologist and Exercise Physiologist, graduated from State University of New York College at Cortland in 1991. He worked as a personal trainer in Beverly Hills and Manhattan Beach, CA, attending the Institute for Psycho-Structural Balancing (IPSB) in Los Angeles in 1994, studying with Erik Dalton. He also studied the Myo-Skeletal Alignment technique for four years as well as studying Active Isolated Stretching (AIS) with Aaron Mattes from 2003 to 2010. In 2014 the VOILÀ Method—a new and innovative way of helping the body heal itself through balancing and harmonizing the body's Keystones during static & dynamic movement to create equilibrium and dynamic kinesthetic stability for increased performance and a pain-free life—was psychically "downloaded" into his consciousness. Today he is the owner of PhysioCareCenter-Injury, Pain, Prevention and Performance Clinic in Los Angeles, California. He also travels the world conducting classes, clinics, workshops and seminars on the VOILÀ Method as well as SOULutions for the Body, Mind & Soul.

He can be reached at www.voilamethod.com

Learning to Listen: A Pathway to Healing

Raised in the tiny town of McDonough, in upstate New York, growing up I was a total jock. Sports were my main focus because I thought they were my ticket out of Tiny Town, USA. I knew my soul would die and waste away if I stayed in that town! In high school I was an All-Star football player. I also played basketball, baseball and ran track. My Mom was the small-town "Doc" and was also on the volunteer paramedic squad. Because the nearest hospital was 20 miles away, when anyone was injured or hurt they would show up at our door at all hours and ask to see if she could take a look at them. Usually each treatment ended with her classic line, "You'll live."

I had no thoughts of becoming a healer. I didn't even know what massage was until many years later when I was personally training a chiropractor to get him into shape and he was helping heal some of my old sports injuries. He told me I might be a really good candidate for massage school—which I actually ended up doing. Turns out I must have inherited my mother's healing instincts because I was a natural and very good at it. Some of the instructors even referred clients to me while I was still in massage school.

But back as a young man, I was just a kid who wanted to play ball. One of the few that went to college to play football from my town, I had an injury-filled career full of cuts and bruises, shoulder separations, a broken ankle, concussion, and muscle pulls—until a major head trauma in college ball ended my career aspirations.

As I look back now, I see that all these injuries

were messages from spirit that I was not following my true purpose. As a young child, I was sensitive to unseen energies and didn't know it. My very first memory was when I was three years old, walking by a rose bush near our back porch. I was wearing a green zip-up hoody and red pants. Suddenly an unfamiliar voice clearly said in my head, "What are you doing here?" Throughout my younger years I would "see" flash images and "hear" high-pitched sounds, but never paid them much attention. Then exactly what I'd seen in the flash image would happen, and each time I wished I had paid more attention!

After college, I became a personal trainer in Beverley Hills, California, then studied massage, later attending the Institute for Psycho-Structural Balancing (IPSB) in Los Angeles, studying with Erik Dalton, and learning the Myo-Skeletal Alignment technique as well as studying Active Isolated Stretching (AIS). As a jock and into fitness, I really enjoyed helping people getting fit and helping with their injuries as a trainer and massage therapist. Most of my clients were coming back from an injury and suffering from pain of some sort—as was I after all my injuries. I'd also had a motorcycle accident that broke my patella (kneecap) and exacerbated my football head trauma. Much of the time I felt I was living in a kind of brain fog. But as much good as I was able to do for my clients, I wasn't able to help and heal myself, which was incredibly frustrating.

I'd been working in the health and fitness field for about 20 years when the big "knock on my door" occurred. My mom passed away from cancer, and she came to visit me the night she passed. She was young and beautiful in the moment. I don't recall any words being spoken. But just her presence triggered something—a Satori moment—a state of consciousness of intuitive illumination. In other words, I woke up! Everything felt and looked the same physically. But everything had changed to a whole new vibration. I felt more open and receptive. I saw things differently than I had in the previous 40 years of living. With New Eyes and New Ears, I finally started listening and paying attention to my intuition, to the voices, to the sounds of Spirit that had always been with me, trying to understand what they meant.

Shortly after I returned home to LA after my mother's funeral, I was working on a client who was experiencing considerable pain. Despite using all the knowledge and tricks I'd gained in 20 years of healing work, nothing helped. Suddenly, out of the corner of my eye, I saw my mom hovering over my left shoulder with her arms crossed, slowly shaking her head, "No." I took a step back, took a deep breath, centered myself, and scanned my client's energy. "Something" —some sense, some awareness—drew my attention to the big toe of her right foot. So, I reached out and made an adjustment to her toe.

Shocked, she said, "I don't know what you just did. But I have no more pain!"

"You've got to be joking!" I replied. "Well, that makes two of us, because I have no idea what I did either."

That night, I was awakened by intense pain in my sacrum/coccyx area. Today, I know that is one of my body-based indicators that I have a message coming in from spirit. That night I simply lay there and started psychically (for lack of a better word) scanning myself as I had with my client that day. My attention was drawn to a certain area of my skull. So I made a slight correction to my skull plates in that area. Instantly, I had no pain and fell back asleep. The message I was being given? Looking back I'd have to say it was a clear, "You're on the right track. Keep going."

Over the course of the next few months the VOILÀ Method of Structural Joint Balancing gradually came to me from that space between sleep and being awake. I would get up in the morning and start remembering a bit of what seemed like a dream of me assessing myself over some sort of physical issue. I would then sit down and try to figure out what I had done in my dream and how it worked. Sometimes I would be awakened in the middle of night with a sudden insight about the body, the body/mind/spirit connection, a certain adjustment, or way to "read" energy. I would run downstairs to the computer to write down my thoughts, sometimes without any understanding of what I was writing, and piece things together the next day or in the days that followed.

This is how the VOILÀ Method was manifested into my consciousness. But it all started with that initial visitation and kickstart from my mother's spirit. After playing and practicing with the information for months, I realized that, not only did my body feel better, my brain fog from all of my severe brain injuries had lifted. What a wonderment!

What Spirit Taught Me About How the Body Works

The body is a pressure unit and all the parts of the body must work in synchronization for maximal results and benefits. Strength should not rely on breath holding or unnatural muscle loading to maintain the pressure for core stability and strength. When the soul, mind, and body are in balance, proper breathing and core stability occur naturally.

The brain, the heart, the gut, the organs, and muscles are major players. But they are just the infantry. They all take their orders from the Soul Source. Once we align the personal self and the body with Spirit and soul, once our "awareness antennae" are in alignment with Spirit and soul for perfect reception, then peace and clarity and self-love flow with purpose like a well-fed river.

Once you align your spiritual sensory antennae, grounding everything you are, balancing experiences and healing wounds from the past (which always hold us back), connecting to the Spirit-Soul Source within, then you can move forward into your purpose with power and grace because you *know who you are*.

The spine

The necessary information for healing lies within the 33 vertebrae of the spine. Yes, we have 33 vertebrae, not just the 24 you were maybe taught about in school. Though limited in movement, much like the cranial bones, the sacrum and the coccyx are also comprised of individual vertebrae. The sacrum does not fully mature until around age

20 and the coccyx not until around 65-70 years of age.

The spine literally tells where the problem is and what needs to be connected or shifted—it holds all the information relating to what old memories are being held, what energies are being blocked, where traumas are stored, what potentials aren't being actualized, what areas of the body need to start communicating with each other—all sorts of information needed for balancing the mind/body/soul/spirit system.

The eyes

The eyes receive and perceive as well as project our perceptions of what we see. They bridge the gap between the multiverse and the perception of what we "see" as reality. There is far more information being taken in than can be absorbed and used by the brain. Most of the 10 million bits of sensory information entering the brain every second come in through the eyes, our largest physical portal. Yet, the eyes can only take in a small sliver of the light spectrum of the multiverse.

We look with our eyes, but we see with our brain. As you can imagine, our brains collect an unbelievable amount of data and cannot process it all. (Actually the brain can only process a maximum of 50-60 bits of sensory data per second—enough to allow us to function here on planet Earth.) Not surprisingly, the brain often misinterprets the incoming data, and it just as frequently ignores incoming data. In fact, studies on inattentional blindness reveal that, depending on our state of awareness and concentration, on average our eyes/brain miss a solid 30 percent of what's in front of us at any given moment! Our brains also "fill in the blanks" with what we want to see or expect to see, constructing perceptions of the world/universe that aren't necessarily real.

Primal brain

The primal brain protects us from perceived danger, whether it's real or perceived. It doesn't know the difference. In fact, the primal brain doesn't know the difference between a mental fantasy and the reality. No wonder we're so stressed! Thinking about a scary situation triggers just as many stress hormones like cortisol to be released into the body as the situation itself. Many people get caught in the fight/flight/freeze loop and don't even know it. This is especially true if they've been subjected to a traumatic event. The event is long over, but the mind, brain and body are still reliving it.

The heart

The heart is our feeling organ, enabling us to receive tremendous amounts of energetic information. It also produces electromagnetic frequencies that, when we're in harmony with our soul and spirit, can actually change the brainwave patterns of other people standing ten feet away without touching them through a dynamic called entrainment. Such is the grace we spread when we're in our Soul-Spirit Space! The heart also nourishes and reenergizes the old patterns of thought and emotion into new healthier patterns.

The shield of fear most people carry around their hearts is the result of a reactionary perceptual pattern holding them back from self-love. And self-love is the primitive origin of love itself.

Unfortunately, in the West, people are taught through religion that it is selfish to love self. And yet, that is the furthest possible thing from the truth! It's the greatest gift you can give yourself. And by loving yourself, you're more capable of loving others.

Connecting to Your Spirit-Soul Space

True healing begins when we can start connecting to our Spirit-Soul Space. Not surprisingly, once people learn about it and embrace the concept, the main thing holding most people back from making this connection is trying too hard. I recall reading *The Way of the Peaceful Warrior* by Dan Millman who travelled the world in search of enlightenment only to find it was right there within himself.

The truth is, *you* are all that is required. When you simply relax and open your mind and heart to allow your spiritual antennae to shift back to the source (Soul/God), there is no need to "work hard" at all. Remember, you didn't have to work hard at shifting your sensing awareness *away* from the source, did you? It just happened.

The Soul Self has no identification with gender. It is neither masculine nor feminine and it is beyond what the mind is capable of knowing and language to express. Becoming receptive to receiving healing information requires getting beyond the polarity of male/female energy dynamics and ego identity, moving into a balanced state.

Basically, male energy is the Destroyer/Hunter/Fixer and female energy is Creator/Nurturer/Supporter. Both are equally powerful and rely on one another. Everyone has both masculine and feminine energies within them. Everyone has both masculine and feminine ego voices within them. And all those illusory polarized thoughts are what keep us from getting to know reality. For example, the masculine ego says, "I can do this on my own. Look at me. Look at what I can do." This is an isolating energy that keeps both healer and patient stuck in their heads, thinking instead of listening, acting instead of being and feeling, thus not hearing the messages from the Spirit-Soul Space clearly, keeping them from receiving the information needed for healing.

Balancing the masculine and feminine energies within to work in harmony with all aspects of being is key to a healthy relationship with self and others—losing the "I, You, Me" to be all one in harmony with all others as we are all connected. This is listening. And as we learn to listen and just "be" connected with our Spirit-Soul Self, we learn to direct our inner antennae to the supreme source within.

To help us do this, it's important to know that the 33 vertebrae of the spine act as the body's physical antenna, gathering information, sending it to the eyes, brain, heart, organs, etcetera. If you know what questions to ask and how to ask the questions using the spine; if you're centered and being in balanced neutrality, keeping masculine and feminine forces within you aligned, listening with clarity, you will tap into your Spirit-Soul Space and tune your antenna to an even higher octave—namely Spirit/ Source/God.

The body is designed to heal itself. It just needs the right information. Healers aren't meant to press their will over their patients' bodies, thinking they know best. The body, hooked up to Spirit/Source, has the answers. A healer's job is to find the answers in their body by tuning in and *listening*. And by "listen," I mean being centered and still and receptive to receiving the information anyway it wants to show up—visually, auditorily, kinesthetically via a pull, heat, tingles, whatever, or through simple direct knowing. When we listen, miraculous things are possible.

It is up to the client to go at their own pace and the client can only go to the level of understanding that the practitioner can open to. It's a two-way street. The dynamic of synergism is key. Which is also why it's so important for the practitioner to be constantly working on his or her own self. Each client you work with has a piece for you and vice versa. We are messengers for each other. It's why we're attracted to see a certain practitioner without knowing why. Many times I have clients say to me, "I have no idea why I am here."

As a two-way information street, if the healer/practitioner isn't aware of their energy and issues and doesn't pay attention, then transference may occur and cause a lot of problems. For example, I had a client come in after having some dental work done. She was experiencing sudden and inexplicable anger and hatred towards men. I "listened" to her body and determined the strong emotions were attached to the jaw and her teeth.

"Is your dentist a woman?" I asked.

"Yes," my client replied.

"Is she going through a bad divorce?"

"Why yes, how did you know?"

Turned out the emotions were not really my client's. They were the dentist's emotions. Yes, my client did have issues around men, which is why the transference was so easy. As I say, everyone we work on is a mirror to self and vice versa.

Another time, a new client came in after having her second knee replacement. She was having pain in the second knee, even after going to physical therapy. The same doctor did both knee surgeries, a year apart. I listened and found the emotions of unworthiness, depression and frustration in the scar of the second knee surgery.

Although my client was indeed frustrated that the second knee replacement didn't go as well as the first one, what I was "hearing" were not my client's emotions. They were the "trapped" emotions of the doctors in the operating room: unworthiness and depression belonged to the main surgeon. The frustration belonged to a different surgeon in the room. After talking with my client's physical therapists, I discovered they were also scratching their heads as to why all their patients from that time period and from that particular group of surgeons were not getting better! Fortunately, I was able to help my client by coaching her to listen and acknowledge the root cause of her pain. Once acknowledged she could express forgiveness and gratitude to the surgeons energetically. From there on her healing rapidly took place.

Opening up to soul's voice has made me the healer I am today. The VOILÀ Method has changed my life. In many ways it saved my life. I was losing my memory, my body hurt all the time, and I had thick brain fog. When I read some blogs and posts I wrote prior to healing through VOILÀ, I am barely able to recognize the language or the person who wrote them. And it was me! It's also changed the way I interact with people. I'm now communicating on a much deeper level than ever before in my life.

By learning to listen and tune into my own Spirit-Soul Space, by retuning my "antennae," by learning to listen to the body—mine and others— it's changed the way I see and hear things. I see connections and the bigger picture. I perceive the structures of the body as very similar in nature. For example, the hand is similar to the foot, just as the cranial bones and the hips are also similar. I see how everything works together. How energy and information flow and how simple things actually are once you balance within yourself. I've learned to love and trust life and love myself. And that's the greatest healing of all.

The Gift

The most healing thing you can do is tap into the primal origin of love, namely love of self. On the journey to self-love it helps to acknowledge and feel gratitude to your ancestors in spirit, as they are there to help guide you along that path. Learn to stop and tune in. Learn to ask questions. Learn to listen. You'll be amazed what you "hear."

A helpful mantra we use in the VOILÀ Method is: "I acknowledge this emotion (whatever it may be) and share it with my highest good (God, the universe, love, light—whatever your belief in a higher power is) with gratitude (try to *feel* the gratitude and forgiveness) for them and myself."

CHAPTER 15

Karen Sailer was born 1962 in the north of Germany. Asked at age 16 what she wanted to be when she grew up, she answered: veterinarian, textile designer, landscaping architect and author. She fulfilled it all, studying veterinarian medicine, then working for seven years as a carpet designer. Moving to Ibiza in Spain, along with her husband, she founded the landscaping company Noahs Garden. Her deep desire to learn the secrets of a happy and healthy life of awareness led her to work with shamans from Native American traditions, Mexico and Peru. The deep connection to her two white soul horses led her on a profound spiritual journey, culminating in the release of films, articles and programmes about the gift horses have to give humanity. She is the founder of Alegria, The Natural Horse and Life Academy for young people. She is author of many articles on holistic gardening and natural horsemanship, as well as the book *Pregnancy: Myth and Reality*. Karen lives with her husband and four sons on a farm in Ibiza, Spain, together with her horses, dogs, cats and a rooster.

She can be reached at www.karensailer.com and www.alegria-ibiza.org

The Magical Journey of Soul Connection

Every human is unique. And every human is born with a gift. It's well sealed and opens up slowly over the years, like a rose.

Even as a little shoot, the rose knows exactly what it wants to be. It's inherent and has nothing to do with thoughts, and that's exactly how it is with you. Your core knows exactly who you are, what your gifts and talents are, what you're good at, which effort is worth it. It's you—it's what you came to Earth with. It's your dream.

As a child I longed for a wild life in nature, for freedom without the limitations growing up in a small German town. Fortunately, I spent a lot of time on the farm of my great-grandmother, Emmy Wetzel. There, between horses, cows, hay, and sweet peas, I found my destiny.

At six years of age I knew you don't find true happiness on the surface, that it lies in the connection with the soul of our planet and all its living creatures. Growing up, I found my spiritual roots in Native American culture. The more I read about Native traditions and the perfection of life, the more I realized how Nature—water, wind, air, fire, sun, earth, plants, animals, stars, and moon— tells us everything we need to know, and the more clearly I saw that almost nobody in Western society teaches children the basic tools for living a happy life.

At age 14, I made a promise to myself: I would never forget how a child feels! I promised to be a different kind of adult, helping young people to understand the world and believe in their dreams.

Now, in my fifties, I am deeply grateful to realize I have kept that promise. But it was a long, arduous journey getting here.

I always wanted a big family, a tribe with lots of children and animals, living the values I believed in. The vison was strong enough to carry me through two marriages and face the dark sides of life. At 33 I moved alone with two little children to Ibiza, Spain where I met my third husband, and all that I had seen in my vision became reality.

We built a farmhouse with a big orchard and lots of animals, and my children grew up as I had always dreamed, in a loving and caring community, where all meet in respect, honouring life in all aspects. But gradually the digital world encroached and my sons retreated with computer games into dark rooms, while the world outside became less and less interesting. I was furious, desperate and overwhelmed. What could I do? What had I overlooked?

Then came three incredibly painful disc prolapses, which I ignored as best as I could—I was good at taking care of others, but not myself—until one day my body was done. The doctors wanted to send me to a special clinic, but I knew what I had to do. My inner voice said loud and clear: "Take one month of rest and rent a house in the mountains of Mallorca."

Being alone was my medicine. I slept when I was tired, ate little, did whatever came into my mind and walked every day in the mountains. After three weeks I had freed my mind and all pain had disappeared. I felt new born and wanted to celebrate the inner changes with something special. I opened the newspaper and there it was: a photo of a young girl with a white horse in an ad for a Spanish stud farm.

The next day I was there to ask for a lesson. But what came out of my mouth was something totally different—words that would change my life. "I want to buy a horse," I said. When they took me to the stables, I walked along the stalls. At the second box, my heart stopped. There stood Xaloc, a five-year-old white Spanish stallion with big black eyes. It was love at first sight.

Everything spoke against my desire to take him home. I had no time and I hadn't ridden for ages. With my back could I ever ride again? But my inner voice was loud. "Do it! He is the best thing that could happen to you. Trust yourself!"

Training

Xaloc arrived in Ibiza and turned my life upside down. He could not be alone and galloped around, whinnying and bucking. I moved my bed into his paddock and slept with him. He calmed immediately. That first night, looking at the stars, listening to his breath, I felt bubbles of joy deep inside my heart whispering, "He is like you. He wants to be free. But he needs partnership. Be free together. That's the secret of true happiness."

I wanted to learn everything I could about his true nature and my own energy. For five months we walked side-by-side through forests and mountains. I became fitter and stronger and he learned to trust me. Then I began to ride. With him I learned to master my life with heart, confidence, discipline, persistence, focus, joy and a feel for opportune moments.

The relationship with my children changed. I learned the qualities of an alpha mare who leads a herd with clear announcements of intent and, if the desired results are achieved, immediate deep calm. I stood up for my values and helped my sons find a balance between the digital world and the world of Nature. I learned how to calm other children's mothers. I learned to be authentic. I learned to be me. I began showing others that it's worth it to be active in the real world, that you can love and master your life and be absolutely honest.

I studied with Chief Sunne Reyna from the Yaqui-Coahuilteka Nations in South California. My first vision quest with him I spent two days and nights on a mountain without water, food and movement, forced to stay within a two-metre wide circle, which I shared with a rosemary bush. I admired the rosemary and all the trees around for their huge patience and endurance. For two days I suffered with them thirst, hunger and the merciless sun. But, unlike them, I could leave the circle and go back to the comfort of my home. In an initiation ceremony the Chief put a talking stick into my hands, decorated with white horse hair. "This stick will guide you to be a voice for children and women." he said. Little did I know at the time what a prophet he was!

The next chapter in Xaloc's and my bid for freedom arrived in the form of a strong, inexplicable pull to go to Peru. I travelled to Cusco and spent a month with a group of Q'ero shamans, working with the spiritual teacher Juan Nunez del Prado, Andean Mystic and anthropologist.

Reality, in the Western world, is based on what we see with our two eyes. But the Q'eros see with *seven* eyes which they are able to open and close by mental focus and inner demand. Seeing the world with seven eyes gives us a holistic view and the ability to connect with all elements and vital forces on our planet and in the entire universe.

The first eye is in the lower back at the sacrum. When we open it, we connect with the water around us. The energy of water can then flow in to clean and purify body and soul and vitalize us with feminine power. The second eye is at the belly button. Here we are connected through a red line with earth. It's a grounding exchange of energy with our true mother and a strong balancing lifeforce. The third eye is at the solar plexus, where we are connected to the sun and the fire. Golden sunrays fill our heart with passion for all we love. The fourth eye is at the throat. It connects us with a silver ray to the air, wind, moon and stars. For the Q'eros, talking the truth with a pure silver voice in compassion is the foundation for authenticity and a balanced social life. The fifth eye is our left eye, with which we see the true nature behind the surface and can focus on specific things. The right eye has the big overview. The seventh eye is the connection to Universe, to our higher self, to God.

The first day Juan led us to Macchu Pichu. Sitting next to him, I asked about the female energies of nature, which the Q'eros call Nustas. He laughed. "They live in all the mountains, plants, rivers, lakes, everywhere. But the Nustas you can only experience yourself." He paused, then pointed. "See the snow-covered mountain over there? That is Wakay Willka, a female mountain. And there, to your right side, you see the river, Willka Nusta. She is female too, as is all water. They have different qualities and gift you with energies which you receive as images or emotions. Call the mountain and the river, connect with both through your eyes and let them touch you."

I started with the mountain, closing my eyes and opening my second eye, imagining a red line between my bellybutton and the mountain. I called and waited. Soon, I felt a soft touch on my left arm. I saw her peak, white glittering snow against a bright blue sky. She was beautiful and proud and she sent me a sound, vibrating in my throat, spreading over my skin and filling all my cells. My body was buzzing. I *was* the mountain! I felt beautiful, glittering, sublime. I was the most beautiful woman in the world.

Giving her my thanks, I shifted attention to the river. I opened my first eye at the sacrum and waited. She touched me on my right arm. Loud laughter sounded within me. *Are you sure that you want it?* she asked with a frothy laugh. I felt how she entered my womb, flowing in swirls through my whole body, cleansing deeply, leaving behind an exuberant joy. I laughed, enjoying the feeling of being a beautiful, wise, cheerful woman. *Like this you have to meet your life*, she said. *Then all will be lighter and more joyful.*

I opened my eyes and saw Juan smiling. "You did well very well. The energies of nature are for free. You will not need therapists to make you feel vital. Just connect to nature. It's pure medicine."

Two years later, I was guided to the Amazon and the master shaman Don Augustin Rivas and his daughter Rosanna Nascimento. The work with them went beyond my imagination. The first Ayahuasca ceremony I was very excited and yet scared to lose control. I drank my glass and sat down. Inside me something expanded. I felt a pressure against my skin, my brain like an inflated balloon. I was scared to death and tried to calm down by breathing. It helped and suddenly I was aware that I could control my fear. With that, I let go and surrendered into the unknown and in the same moment the pressure inside gave way to a new sensation: I expanded out of my body into the room.

I was an empty vessel, connected to everyone around me. I heard the others suffering, some cried, others vomited. I felt all their emotions without any attachment. It was a constant flow of emotions and my heart was full with love and compassion. Knowing that we are all one was not anymore a theory. It was reality.

During all of the many ceremonies, I had no heavy physical or psychological reactions and no processing of traumas or fears. Instead, each ceremony gave me a deep insight into the interconnections of life, leaving me with a deep gratitude for living on our planet—gratitude that remains with me today. I travelled to the stars and saw our beautiful planet from outside, floating in the giant universe, a paradise in the middle of darkness. I saw life within all things, each chair, stone, and leaf was a breathing being, connected through patterns of light. I communicated with animals and used the ceremonies to talk to Xaloc. I called him and he came into my visions and showed me how he wanted to be with me. He danced around me and invited me to play.

In the jungle it became clear that Xaloc was with me, even when he was physically absent. Both Rossa and Don Augustine saw a white horse at my side—the guardian of my soul. In my shamanic journeys I learned to see him and understand his messages, which were always about freedom and trust. He came in my dreams and touched me with his nose on parts of my body that needed my attention. He blew his warm breath into my heart when I was sad. Over time, dreams and reality intermingled and we communicated on invisible channels, beyond time and space.

Years later, when he was almost twenty years old, I developed a big myoma—a fibroid tumour in my uterus—and needed surgery. After I got back from the hospital I heard that when I was taken into surgery he retreated to the stables and stood there motionless for five hours, his head to the wall, completely withdrawn. He was with me and gave me his strength until I woke up.

Passing the Wisdom On

The deeper I connected to Xaloc, the more painful it became to see the way people treated their horses. Locked up in small, lightless stables, lonely and without any contact with other horses, many were malnourished and afraid of the violent training methods that were commonly used by their masters. Cruel whips and bits were the least of it. Their lives were enormously sad, their fate shared by millions of other horses on our planet.

My best friend, veterinarian Dr. Martina Czolgoszewski, and I founded a charity and rescued many. But the real problem was that the awareness of people didn't change. The stables filled up again and again with new misery. I meditated and asked my spirits for help. Slowly, pictures rose in me. I saw Xaloc and me performing at big shows. I saw children playing with horses, conquering the hearts of audiences. Again my inner voice spoke: *Think outside the box. Don't think what you can do against the misery, but what you can do for it. Turn it over in joy and people will follow you.*

Joy was the key and suddenly I knew what to do. I wanted to start with children and show them how these wonderful beings feel, how they learn, and how they work in joy with us. How shared joy is real joy. At the same time the desire grew to start my own school. Thus Alegria, a Natural Horse & Life Academy for young people, was born.

Alegria is the Spanish word for joy, for the tingling sensation we feel at the sight of beauty and balance—the tingling which horses naturally evoke by their very presence! Excited, I approached the local public stables with an idea. Each Saturday I would teach children in natural horsemanship and after seven weekends we would have a horseshow and they would demonstrate to an audience what they had learned.

I worried that the children and the school horses, who were often dull and anxious, would not learn and trust very quickly, let alone be able to captivate a large audience. But I poured all my wisdom about energy, awareness and connection learned from shamans and my horse masters into the lessons. Seven Saturdays later, the first show was a big success. Within three years we managed to change a large number of people's awareness about horses in an entertaining way.

And yet, the moment I opened the school, a change began in me. It felt like a chapter was ending. I had fulfilled the promise to my horse and to all horses. I should have been happy. But instead a longing grew. Once again I was searching without knowing for what. I prayed for guidance and trusted that something new would show up. Three months later, I met a man.

You know the feeling when you meet someone from a past life? You look into each other's eyes and everything is there in one go. In our case, it was not just familiarity and physical desire, but also fear of something that I could no longer control. After a short intense relationship, we decided that our ways must separate again. His farewell present was something very special: a small equestrian figure carved in stone he had found buried in the ground in France. She was very old, and despite the male warrior clothes, I sensed she was female. Whenever I took her in my hand I felt a heartbeat, like from a small bird.

She wanted to tell me something. I meditated with her and always carried her with me. But the only thing she revealed was that she came to me to work with women. I trusted that the way would show itself—and it showed itself through sadness. As an inner sadness grew, a knot began to grow in my left breast. Breast cancer! It was a shock, but I got the warning message. The left breast represents injured femininity and I knew that I had much to heal in myself and much to do to help my sisters on this Earth to heal past and present injustices. After the tumour was removed, I healed myself with medicinal plants from the Amazon with the help of my shaman Rosanna. It was a deep cleansing and slowly I rose like a phoenix from the ashes.

Xaloc accompanied me through this difficult time. As the lump in my left breast grew, he injured his left hind leg. A muscle tore and healed so badly that he limped. It was clear that I could not ride him anymore. I asked him if he wanted to tell me something and the answer touched and saddened me deeply: "It is time for you to find a successor for me."

It was hard for me to follow his words, but slowly a desire began to take shape. More and more often I thought of Portugal and its horses, the Lusitanos. I made contact with a woman who could help me in my search for my new horse. I told her my wishes and expectations and received her message a week later: "I found him!"

Habanero, she said, was a four-year-old, beautiful, white stallion. "He's perfect—except for a deep scar across his nose." My heart raced at her words. I felt an old memory rising in me and with it the feelings I had for the man who gave me the equestrienne figure: magical attraction and the fear of something big that I could not control. I asked Rosanna and my astrologer for advice and both said the same thing: "Habanero is connected to you through a past life. He came back to do a mission with you. With him you will enter a new dimension."

In a ceremony with Rosanna, I fell into a deep trance and went back to the time when the figure was made. I was a warrior in France at the time of the Huguenot war in the 16th century—a woman who, hidden in men's clothes, went to war with her white stallion to fight injustice against women and children. The stallion had a war injury—a deep scar on his nose. When I was wounded, he carried me, unconscious, to a castle. There I was healed and met the lord of the castle. It was he who had the figurine made to remind him of me after I left.

He died with it in his hand, standing in a field not far from the castle ... the same field my lover in this life found the carving.

The universe is a giant narration and everyone has their own story in it. Souls are connected, across distant times and places, and find themselves again when their time comes. I have found my soul horse again and with him a new, yet so old dream. Now I am dedicated to the next stage of life—dedicated to women and the awakening of the feminine power we need more than ever today.

The feminine side in each human is about trusting our inner guide, flowing with life, forgiving in emotional strength, feeling the elements inside us, living with the rhythm of nature, knowing that we are connected to the universe and all life around us. So has begun my next project—the Wild Heart Programme to awaken and empower the inner wildness of women—to teach women to find out who they really are and to find their spiritual roots. Wild Heart also has special programs for women with horses to connect on a deeper level of understanding beyond riding techniques and the different areas of horsemanship.

To be in our wild hearts, we must have the courage to be true to ourselves. Then we are all free.

The Gift

Growing up we learn that daily showering and teeth brushing are important for hygiene. But no one tells us what to do with all the rubbish that gathers in our minds and hearts. Sometimes we are so filled with bad news, worries for our planet and disputes with friends we think we're going to choke on it.

From my journey with the Q'ero Indians in the Peruvian Andes, I brought back a very effective technique to help clean spirit and soul. It's so simple at first glance it might seem useless. But don't be fooled!

The Q'eros don't judge energy. They don't separate it into good and bad, but rather assess it as light and heavy. Light, pure energy comes from the universe and is available at any time for us to recharge. It feels like warm summer rain. Heavy energy can only be produced by humans. Animals and plants can't do it. And everybody knows how it feels. "I have a heavy heart. I feel heavy as lead," are things we say often.

This heavy energy comes from things we encounter daily that burden us and can't be digested. It's not good for us and has to be removed from the body. But guess what? There's a natural energy cycle to everything. Nothing goes to waste. Planet Earth is actually nourished by our heavy energy. For her it's light and sweet. A real delicacy. So, don't worry about defiling Mother Earth with your soul garbage! Earth is happy to help, ensuring your heavy energy is released back into the big cycle of life.

If you do the following exercise every day then you won't be caught up in yourself. You will feel lighter and freer. You'll be able to see the things that disturb you with different eyes. You will become strong and capable, instead of being a victim of your sorrow.

Practice:

Stand on the earth and imagine a hole opening on the top of your head. Request the light energy to flow inside you. Only a little thought is required and it will happen. Let it flow into every single cell to the tips of your fingers and toes. Then open a hole in the soles of your feet and ask the heavy energy to leave your body. Again, only the thought is needed.

Let everything out that you no longer need: Pain, tension, harsh thoughts, everything that weighs you down. Earth will happily accept and take care of the disposal. After that, seal your soles again and carry on letting light energy into your body, until you feel lighter. Now, close the hole on your head, be grateful for the cleanse and begin your day.

CHAPTER 16

Tatyana Rae von Knobelsdorff received her earliest shamanic training at the feet of her paternal great-grandmother, Nana. Tatyana's father was of the Lipan Apache people from the Mexican states of Chihuahua, Nuevo Leon, and Coahuila. The skills associated with shamanism were passed to her from her father, and now to her son, Zachary, who is being groomed in the Remembering. In addition to her family apprenticeship, she apprenticed with don Miguel Angel Ruiz, Sr. for sixteen years. Tatyana's mastery is ceremonial Dreaming, and the Prayer of Intention.

She received her MA in Psychology at the University of California Fullerton, opening her own practice, specializing in addiction. She taught at The Canyon of Malibu Rehabilitation Center, bringing their clientele the Wisdom of the Elders, their bridge to Spirit. She is a co-founder of the Temple Called Beautiful, an organization dedicated to the channeling of the Masters, and was initiated as a High Priestess in the Order of Saint Germaine.

For the last eighteen years Tatyana has been working with individual clients worldwide. She also conducts workshops and seminars.

She can be reached at TatyanaRae.com

Relearning the Art of Living: Naked Bliss

Sensuality is Divine Romance in action, the art of experiencing one's self *as* Life—intoxicated with the width and breadth, vibrancy and variety of existence—melting into the warmth of the sun, drunk on the night's perfume, sipping on moonlight, fiercely loving ourselves.

Sensuality cannot be described as a thing, but rather as an affair, a tryst with one's senses, along with a profound yearning to always be receiving more and more. It is a sensitivity, an awareness of the mood, of the resonance that we create moment-to-moment as conscious beings within the Universe. We are designed to be obsessed with the love call within our own hearts, constantly seeking to reunite with Breath, with each other, with Life, *with God.*

It is with this body and its ability, its talent, its raw awareness, that we begin to understand existence. It is with this body and its refined sensibilities and capacity to feel and energetically navigate life that we learn. By paying attention to what surrounds us, we begin to develop our other senses of intuition, discernment, and knowing. These highly developed senses let us know immediately when we have transgressed against ourselves and when we are accepting anything that is less than harmonious and aligned with our true "self."

Unfortunately, for several thousand years we have been told that we are only human, that we are not perfect, that we come into life with original sin. We have been crippled by various cultures and institutions giving us the mixed message that we are beautiful, but vain if we acknowledge it. That we are intelligent, but arrogant if we attempt to use it. That we are talented, but conceited if we believe it.

We have learned to make ourselves small in order to fit in and survive, to quench our fire, our enthusiasm and our sensuality. And yet it is through these bodies—these blessed sensed-based vehicles—that we reclaim the preciousness, the glory and perfection of the Divine working not just through us, but as us.

The Body is Divine

This was never more apparent to me than when I worked at The Canyon in Malibu. The Canyon is a drug and alcohol treatment center that often ends up serving those who have been physically injured, succumbing to addiction to drugs and/or alcohol during the pain management stage of their injury.

The Canyon employed me to introduce a new understanding to the clientele about why they might be choosing to medicate their feelings, numbing the pain that was in their minds as well as their bodies. It was during an evening class that I—along with everybody else in the group—was granted the privilege of observing God as human expressing through the Body Beautiful.

That particular evening the class was attended predominantly by athletes, so I asked the group, "Why are you an athlete? Why such a hazardous career? Why, with all the pain your sport inflicts on your body, do you return to it again and again?"

I gazed at the young men surrounding me—all in their prime, injured, and now held captive by chemicals that had become a necessity to their well-being. My eyes rested on one young man in particular. He seemed intrigued, skeptical, but eager to consider my question. Is that a flicker of light I see in the hollows of his eyes? I wondered.

He was a snowboarder. An X-game snowboarder whose sport demanded being helicoptered high into vast wildernesses still retaining their virgin snow, pristine, untouched even to sight. I gave him the floor and he began talking, not directly about snowboarding at first, but about the relationship he had with anticipation. How he looked forward to dressing before a ride, his final glance back as he boarded the chopper, his ride up into the mountains. His voice was soft, awkward, hesitating, as if revealing intimate details of a recent affair. He shared how his stomach would knot, knowing it was going to be a wild and dangerous ride. Then he spoke of the moment of being released.

"Released?" I asked.

"Yeah, the pilots get you as close to the ground as they can. But you still gotta drop your board and jump," he said, with a brash tone of pride. Then he leaned forward in his chair ... and Spirit spoke.

In uninhibited detail he offered the group his connection to a Living God. As he shared, the room became a sanctuary, a sacred space. He spoke of his feelings just before the drop, how a surge of gratitude would flood his body and he would know everything was going to be fine. With touching reverence, he described pushing off, how, as the downhill momentum gathered, his joy increased to the point that he could feel himself disappearing into his bliss, which was, in turn, the living bliss of the snow, the incline, and the mountain.

His voice became animated and excited, full of longing and tenderness. He said he no longer existed—that he could hear God singing through the wind, the trees, and the swish-swishing of his board. His body not only knew what to do, it became an instrument through which all Creation joined together with him...as him. By the end of his account his eyes shone like the crystallized water he was so fond of.

He had remembered his Body's love of living—as his own.

The Work of Love

I hesitate to talk about healing, because humanity doesn't need healing. We are perfect just the way we are. At least as we were created...

We are not sick, crazy, or broken. We are, instead, grieving, lonely, shamed and defeated. Domestication has demanded that we sever our bond with our instincts, that we forfeit our relationship with our common sense and intuition, that we forgo our ecstasy. But we long for the intercourse of our senses. We hunger for beauty and desperately desire to know what we embody. To feel that all is well. Yet that cannot happen until we make room for our surroundings, our environment, our condition as human through our bodies. Beauty and grace, health, will forever elude us until we embrace life itself as our lover.

I do not present myself as Shaman. I don't even use the word. I present to my clients and the world as a human—a human representing life as God. I will not be put into a category, into a box for the convenience of someone's understanding. I am a disruptor to those around me because I no longer fear being tamed. Instead I dance between the lines. I live between the bones. I glide in and out of your breath.

We are a triumvirate: Me, my Body, and God. And so are you.

Each time we make this acknowledgment, an inner alignment takes place. Our bodies rejoice as the holy vehicles they are, delightedly translating sensations as the voice of God, the eyes of God, the hands of God, the skin and nose and ears of God. The body trembles in anticipation of experiencing everything—and so do I.

I find that the greatest fear my clients have is losing their inhibitions. Many of them have actually voiced this, saying, "If I lose my inhibitions, well, Tatyana, I might strip myself of my clothes and run down the street naked!"

And I say, "Don't worry!" Losing inhibition is just a metaphor for the ecstasy that you would feel upon remembering and rekindling your relationship with yourself as life. Unfortunately, we have come to fear the energy that courses through our bodies, quickening our heartbeat at the sight of our Beloved, commanding our surrender during lovemaking.

I cannot think of a better example of this than my client Emily. Upon meeting her, one is struck by her quiet, introspective manner, a countenance that tends to feel distant and removed. In our work together we concentrated on releasing the effervescent 'Pixie' that she kept tucked away, whose absence inhibited her ability to participate and enjoy, to feel contented or satisfied with daily life. But occasionally, without warning, out would emanate the most hilariously captivating giggles and guffaws—the only indicator that the 'Pixie' was alive and well.

Then came the posting on Facebook...Emily had run a full marathon in Portland, Oregon. In that cold, damp, dreary weather she had run, and a photograph was taken of her within minutes of finishing. She was radiant, beaming with joy, overcome by health and wellbeing. For the first time I saw the Pixie in all her glory: Emily's uninhibited, unguarded, truest self-expression. Caught on camera, she could never again tell me she didn't feel, that she only knew depression and self-doubt. That photograph had captured her running down those streets naked, as herself, stripped of all self-doubt. Naked, for Emily, was jubilance.

Emily is now into pole dancing...

So, how do I know that we are intended to experience the heights of pleasure and joy, to have feelings flutter through our cells like butterflies on a summer's day? To anticipate the taste of freshly baked bread, its aroma slyly arousing our memories of family, hearth and home, love and safety, good friends and good times? How do I know that being present to our feelings, our body's language, is the pathway to bliss?

I learned this the hard way. Like Emily, once upon a time in this form that I call my own, I was caught within the confines and ritualization of socialized domestication. I was incapable of being in the flow of my own feelings, ignoring the wisdom that attempted to filter through my daily life and tasks. I became frightened of shedding my inhibitions. Like so many uncounted millions of other people, I was angry, bitter, and resentful. I, too, was pretending amnesia. And it was killing me.

How It happens

My mother said I learned to walk and kiss at the same time. The story goes that for many days I went around kissing *everything* my wobbly legs could carry me to. Chair legs, table legs, my toys, nothing was immune to my delight of kissing. But what made my mother and father laugh most was the fact that I found the greatest pleasure in kissing my own hands. Ahhhh, sensation ...

On my father's side I am Apache, from the borders of what is known today as Texas and at one time Northern Mexico. My paternal great-grandmother, my father, myself, and now my youngest son, Zachary, are Shaman. My mother was from Mexico City and her family are Curanderas (healers) My mother had the gift of healing hands and the ability to see within a person's resistances. People came from miles around to just "be" with my Mother, for she exuded absolute conviction that "all is well." My mother's ability was not so much to heal, but to restore faith in one's health.

Much wondrous, magical lore was passed to me. Recipes for wisdom, tranquility and peace, prescriptions against diseases of the heart and mind, and soul. My instruction was accomplished through the *Arts of Discipline and Correction.* My every move was monitored for preciseness. I was trained in self-awareness, learning through heightened senses to become one with every situation, able to immerse myself seamlessly in my environment in order to disappear energetically.

How I walked ... was I being noisy, clumsy, bumping into surrounding objects? How I opened or closed doors. Did I turn the knob all the way or did I tug and wrestle with the door? Was the door pulled closed gently behind me? I was also directed to be aware of the actions of others. My Nana and I would sit quietly and watch people, observing minute details, items of clothing wrong side out, mismatched socks, articles of clothing soiled, spotted, or torn, how their bodies lurched and lunged instead of a steady grace-filled gait.

Living was an art in my great-grandmother's home. It could be seen in the way she never spilled anything when serving or being served. Anything she did, she did with sincere attention and appreciation. I was taught to fold clothes, laying the garment out flat, stroking the wrinkles away, bringing the raw edges inside, only the smoothness of the article left to your sight. Ugh! Absolute torture for a child, but absolutely necessary to teach patience, observance, flow, and beauty.

I learned how to tell the differences in the energies of objects, animate and inanimate. I learned that everything is alive. When my grandmother was cooking she would hand me a bunch of cilantro, asking me what it had to "say." I would make up silly stories, saying thing like, "It says it's yummy." She never scolded me, she just gave me that "look." Eventually I learned the cilantro, the tomatoes, the gardening tools, the worms eating the tomatoes, they all had something to say. With time, I became fascinated by their stories, the ones Nana could hear. But to hear their stories, first I had to get quiet, holding very still, waiting respectfully. Even the hoe sang its song, had its medicine.

With this kind of upbringing, I can imagine you wondering, "How did she lose her way when she had this kind of training, connection, and appreciation for life growing up?"

My answer is this: we don't all have the training I was given, but we *all* have this same appreciation for life in the beginning as little children until the exuberance and joie de vivre is programmed out of us. One way or another, we are domesticated.

And then there was the natural rebelliousness of youth.

I listened, I learned, I respected. But I chafed at the insinuations my elders made about the corruption, the infection, the sickness that pervaded the mainstream society I was born into. How was I to enter a world I was being taught had nothing to do with "us?" To my mind, it seemed we were really just like "them"—drawing distinctions, separating, biased, prejudiced, exclusionary.

The stock answer, "This is the way it has always been..." grew too familiar. I was taught to be observant, and what I observed was judgments and opinions holding more weight than simple observation. A great deal of superstition also made its way into my world. There were foods that shouldn't be eaten while menstruating. Spirits from other worlds seeking host bodies. I rebelled against it all.

Observation of others began to feel like superiority. Superstitions began to feel like fear. Our world of tradition and the modern world were both the same, filled with philosophies, dogmas, rules and regulations. Disturbed, I found myself retreating, slowly backing away.

I attended the University of Fullerton in California, graduating with a Master's Degree in Psychology, modern man's equivalent of Shamanism. But I found myself at odds with my professors. In my labs and clinics I noticed a high number of people who obviously qualified as empaths—people who, to my shamanic-trained eye, were simply over-loaded with too much outside stimulation—being medicated and placed in analysis. I respectfully asked why we would not try to detoxify their bodies first, in order to reset their clock so to speak and calm them down. But there was such a smugness in the medical world, an arrogance that would allow only what was known from books and intellectual processes. Keeping their protocols intact seemed far more important than the facts concerning the individual client.

My counseling practice turned out to be equally disheartening.

Western humanity's indoctrination is complete in its devastation. The undermining of our instincts and our joy is thorough. It begins the moment we can understand the word "other," the moment we start to see others and life as something separate from "me." From that point onward we are left with a dull, incessant disquiet, a feeling of refinement lost, of beauty misplaced, of connections broken. I witnessed this disquiet in every person, young or old, who came to me for 'healing'. Their spirits, their hearts, were mostly intact. But a vitality—the Light—was missing from their eyes.

These people were silently disappearing, fading away. Yet most showed little interest in doing the real work necessary to come back to life. Few people genuinely desired a life lived without deceit or cunning. They weren't interested in learning how to question, to notice, to see how their lives were reflections of inattention, avoidance, deflection and programming. They just wanted a magic pill to make them feel better while they clung to their internal stories and programming—that was sapping the juice from their veins.

I let my practice go. For seven years I floundered, disoriented and bewildered, beset by doubts, struggling to make sense of my world. It was at this point that I met don Miguel Angel Ruiz, Sr., who mentored me through this period of reconstruction. His approach was basically to deepen my process of self-examination and questioning. For fourteen years I learned to question *everything*, from the sublime to the ridiculous, from the food I ate to the beliefs of my elders, from the clothes I wore to the morals and ethics of society, government and religion.

Take monogamy as an example. Did I practice it because of a lack of confidence? Because without it I feared my partner would be free to find someone better? Was it because I didn't want to go to hell? Or did I just enjoy focusing on one relationship at a time?

Over and over I was forced to answer one essential question: Was my choice fear or freedom based? I began to remember and apply all that I had learned watching the behavior of others with my father or great-grandmother. I slowed my daily pace down. I took time to admire my sons, their features, the differences in the sound of their laughter or the exact color of their eyes. I took pleasure gazing out my sunroof while at a stop light. I rekindled my love of solitude and the peace it carries.

Slowly, I picked up the jewels hiding in both shamanism and psychology—at least the ones that sparkled for me—and I returned to my work, to my self without restrictions.

The Body Cannot Lie

Wisdom is a process of learning from our mistakes. And our biggest mistake—the mistake that is leading modern humanity into depression, addiction, and self-destruction—is not trusting our bodies. The body cannot lie. Never. Our feelings, registering in the body moment to moment, are a constant compass telling us exactly what to do and where to go, what is healthy and what is unhealthy for us. But we have to pay attention to our feelings to create harmony within.

The body knows what is appropriate for it to eat and drink, to wear and drive. We know when a job or a situation or a person doesn't feel right and when they do. Our sense of touch, our sight, our sense of smell, all guide us in a healthy direction. However, we have been so programmed into self-denial, so overwhelmed with constant stimulation, that not only do we refuse to listen to our inner promptings, we can no longer hear them. We refuse to practice discipline or govern and regulate our minds.

The majority of my clients do not need counseling, they need a grandmother whose arched eyebrow and silent stare means, "Look again"—a swift check-in with the facts right in front of them. For example, Darius was a passionate, highly energetic, motivated man who seemed to have "lost his tongue." For him, life was a matter of controlling what he termed anger, an anger he never acted on. I worked with him, helping him identify what he was actually feeling moment to moment. I gave him exercises that required his vigilance, tracking his day, noticing and labeling his feelings within different situations.

Through self-observation, Darius began to see that he had no boundaries, no opinions, no rights. He realized the exuberance and vitality he had exhibited as a male child had been frowned upon, he had learned to be quiet and do as he was told. He had been squashed. Gradually, he realized there was seldom anger within him, just the uncomfortable tension that arose when he wouldn't allow himself to express his genuine feelings in different situations. He had assumed he was always angry, when instead he was simply experiencing heightened body tension from too much self-judgment and self-control.

I won't say he is now a non-stop chatterbox, but the skill with which he can share his feelings and his high energy are now in alignment.

My client Molly was terrified that she could not keep her daughter safe. (Safety was extremely important to her because of her own childhood.) She started hallucinating about break ins and car accidents, kidnapping and illnesses.

I asked her to sit quietly and listen to her child while she slept, to listen for her breathing patterns, to watch how often she stirred, to notice any favoritism she showed in sleeping positions. By paying strict, quiet, attentive attention, Molly discovered that her love and appreciation had been overshadowed by her fear-based projections. She discovered she adored this little creature and that she had misinterpreted deep concern for the feeling of fear, based on her own childhood.

When we learn to accurately identify our feelings, when we learn to be quiet and listen internally, we find stability and safety in ourselves. When we learn to trust our inner feelings we gradually learn to trust our outer senses as well. And when that happens, the magic of life returns. Smells become fragrances, tastes become savoring, sight becomes art, and sounds become music. And touch? Oh Lordy! Touch becomes intoxication— the silk under your fingers, the smoothness of your lover's thigh, feeling her hair cascading upon your face and chest, cuddly little animals, soft and warm and furry, feeling the frost beneath your fingertips, your breath misting like fog in the air. Fully restored to our bodies' senses, a communion occurs. The reconnection is made. The fear and aloneness drop away and we are whole once more.

This world, this life, is nothing less than a physical rendezvous with God, the Lover of all Lovers. We need no rules, no regulations, no instructions, no healing to experience life and our divinity. We were born to do this. To *feel* this. To experience the pleasure of having the companionship of our bodies as friend, lover, temple, reflection ... as God.

The Gift

Here is my prayer for you. Repeat it daily, or as many times as you need to, reminding yourself of who you really are.

May there be nothing between me and myself as God, not even a membrane. Naked Bliss...

RESOURCES

Recommended reading:

- *Awakening to the Spirit World: The Shamanic Path of Direct Revelation* by Sandra Ingerman and Hank Wesselman
- *Historical Atlas of World Mythology* by Joseph Campbell
- *Of Water and Spirit* by Malidoma Patrice Somé
- *Plant Spirit Shamanism: Traditional Techniques for Healing the Soul* by Howard Charing and Ross Heaven
- *Soulcraft: Crossing into the Mysteries of Nature and Psyche* by Bill Plotkin
- *Soul Retrieval* by Sandra Ingerman
- *The Jaguar That Roams the Mind* by Robert Tindall
- *The Secrets of the Talking Jaguar* by Martin Prechtel
- *The Way of the Shaman* by Michael Harner
- *The Woman in the Shaman's Body, Reclaiming the Feminine in Religion and Medicine* by Barbara Tedlock
- *Wazuriri & Shaman del Rio* (River Shaman) by Cayo Vasquez

Also by our authors

- *Awaken the Inner Shaman* by José Luis Stevens, Ph.D
- *Encounters With Power* by José Luis Stevens, Ph.D
- *Lori: The Disintegration of My Ordinary Reality* by Lori Morrison
- *The Shamanic Way of the Bee* by Simon Buxton
- *Through the Rabbit Hole: Explore and Experience the Shamanic Journey and Energy Medicine* by Jan Engels-Smith
- *Dancing In The Unknown* – Rebecca Haywood, Wayne D. Carter, Joel Crandall

Videos:

- *The Way of the Shaman: The Work of Michael and Sandra Harner* https://www.youtube.com/watch?v=JNloOTQoRzA
- *Ur-Musig* - Eine Reise durch die Klanglandschaften der Innerschweiz und des Appenzellerlandes. Available at http://www.ur-musig.ch
- *Vanishing of the Bees*

Movies:

- Noah
- The Emerald Forest

CPSIA information can be obtained
at www.ICGtesting.com
Printed in the USA
BVHW09s2306221018
530946BV00016B/305/P